Quit Everything

Quit Everything

Interpreting Depression

Franco "Bifo" Berardi

Published by Repeater Books

An imprint of Watkins Media Ltd

Unit 11 Shepperton House

89-93 Shepperton Road

London

N1 3DF

United Kingdom

www.repeaterbooks.com

A Repeater Books paperback original 2024

1

Distributed in the United States by Random House, Inc., New York.

ISBN: 9781915672513

Ebook ISBN: 9781915672520

Printed and bound in the United Kingdom by TJ Books Limited

MIX
Paper from
responsible sources
FSC® C013056

Contents

Introduction:
Desertion as Ethics
and Strategy

In the spring of 2022, when Russian tanks invaded Ukrainian territory and the majority of the Ukrainian population resisted the invasion with unexpected energy, slowing down the advance of Russian troops and winning support from European opinion, I wondered what I would have done if I had been a resident of Kyiv.

When the war broke out, I felt unable to take a position in favor of one or the other of the two contenders, because the reasoning of both implied destructive and unacceptable projects. The rhetoric of liberal democracy represented the interests of Western financial capitalism, while the rhetoric of Russian national sovereignty represented the interests of a brutal oligarchic class. It was therefore impossible for me to take a position on the political level, but an ethical question arose with painful urgency.

The dynamics of war are a chain of unavoidable automatisms that eradicate the residual margin of freedom that individuals can enjoy. This chain of automatisms has the effect of blowing up other automatisms — like energy and food supply infrastructures — one after the other.

What is the meaning of the word "ethics" under these conditions? Is it possible to choose ethically from among the deadly designs that the great world powers project on the future of the world? There is not.

Then I asked myself a more radical question: Does the word "ethics" mean anything at all? Is there a sphere of knowledge and action that can properly be defined by the term "ethics"? In the end I came to the conclusion that it is possible to define the concept of ethics only in relation to other concepts from the fields of anthropology, psychology, and politics.

Ethics (as conscience and as action) means making choices between rationally undecidable alternatives. When we have to choose on the basis of an intelligent calculation, there is no ethical judgment, just intellectual discrimination. But when we cannot make a rational choice on the basis of certain and calculable data, when the choice must be made between undecidable alternatives, then we speak of an ethical choice. At such a conjuncture, intelligence is no longer an appropriate tool. Instead, consciousness — self-reflective thought — helps to make a choice between the undecidable alternatives.

Therefore, after having reflected at length on the possibility of a political choice (as if something depended on this decision of mine), I said to myself, "Don't worry, you don't have to choose, you don't have to do anything, because nothing can be done." As there is nothing to be done, the only thing I can do is think.

I started writing this book in March 2022, as if it were the map of a hallucination, because there was no better way to understand chaos and happily process both my despair and the despair surrounding me. It is a map of the abyss in which the whole of human kind is participating, but also a map of possible lines of escape: a different way to see what we see; a different interpretation of depression, of passivity, of exhaustion.

Reflecting on the many wars that are devastating the planet, the multi-dimensional concept of desertion emerged in full view, and I saw it as poised to become a strategically effective model, not only on the field of war. Desertion is a way to escape the horrors of war, but also a way to escape the horrors of peace.

To desert means to abandon the battle, somehow sneak out of the fray, weasel away from the place where the fight is raging, and flee, before the military police catch you and shoot you in the back for your cowardice. Desertion is becoming the line of conduct of more and more people in more and more fields of contemporary life.

I praise this behavior. Flight, abandonment, inaction, desertion are the only behaviors that I consider ethically acceptable and strategically rational. Defeatism, sabotage.

When I realized that devastation — of the physical environment, of the soul — has reached a point of no return, when I realized that techno-financial automatisms have disabled democracy and political action itself, I came to the conclusion that desertion is the only ethically sustainable position, and also the only strategically effective behavior.

At that point, the problem of subjectivity appeared in different light.

Subjectivity in an Era of Regression

The political history of modernity, including the history of the labor movement and the revolutionary movements of the twentieth century, is based on the tacit premise of progress, on the idea that the future entails expansion: expansion of the production base, expansion of markets, expansion of consumption. This premise made the integration of society possible, despite uncountable conflicts.

Political subjectivity in the various phases of the century was, however, always conceived within an expansive perspective: the communist project, which we had considered the culmination of modern history, was conceived of as an abolition of capitalism, but it was also the full deployment of the capitalist tendency to increase labor productivity thanks to machines. Therefore the possibility of a communist future moved in the same expansive direction as the history of capitalism: it was the final leap in the deployment of the power of technology, but also the autonomization of technology from the form of capital.

However, the pandemic, global civil war, and the acceleration of climate collapse have marked the end of this expansive paradigm, forcing us to imagine the events to come from the perspective not of expansion, but of exhaustion and contraction. In the background, extinction emerges as a possible outcome, so that we have to find lines of escape.

Since the end of the twentieth century (since the publication of the *Report on the Limits to Growth* by the Club of Rome in 1972), awareness of the exhaustion of resources and limits to growth has been growing and growing. After the oil shock of the 1970s, capitalism emerged from crisis by relaunching profits through technological advances that enabled an intensification of productivity and an acceleration in the circulation of information. Neoliberalism then broke the constraints that had slowed down intensification: regulations, social resistance, the eight-hour working day, rest for cognitive workers, and so forth.

Capital thus managed to counter the fall in the rate of profit with a double movement: on the one hand, the use of financial dynamics made possible an upward redistribution of the wealth produced, bringing with it the impoverishment of society and increasing concentration of capital; on the other, the acceleration of labor productivity, especially of cognitive work. The extreme intensification of productivity and the exploitation of mental energies have coincided with the passage from the territorialized form of industrial production to the intensive digital form in the semio-capital sphere.

But this intensification cannot hold beyond a certain point.

First of all, the intensification of the productive rhythm, linked with the acceleration of the information cycle, caused chaos in the collective mind. At the same time, the intensification of extraction has accelerated the trend towards environmental catastrophe. The culmination of neoliberal reform is therefore Chaos — the systemic ungovernability of social, productive, and distributive processes.

Chaos continuously disrupts the social integration made possible by the techno-linguistic automatisms that hold together the cycles of production, distribution, and information. The set of these technical automatisms that employ artificial intelligence tends to configure a cognitive Automaton that must continually mend the breaking points, the explosions of chaos.

Automata and Chaos have grown together in a dynamic balance that has now reached a breaking point: psychotic disorder of the social mind.

The acceleration of the information cycle and the intensification of cognitive activity result in chaos and jeopardize the functioning of the collective mind, spreading panic and depression where capital needs energy and recombinable order. The fragments of cognitive activity are increasingly dissociated and incompatible, less and less recombinable, and more and more chaotic: mass psychosis, demented violence, and war are not provisional phenomena, and we don't have a therapy for mass psychosis. So the psychotic condition is becoming a systemic one, as exposed by the dynamics of the Ukrainian War.

For the first time we have to acknowledge an unstoppable tendency towards the disintegration of the solidarity on which the social bond is founded. The neo-reactionary movements that have grown over the last decade as a global alternative to liberal democracy are an effect of this regression, of this unthinkable, and therefore unthought-of, contraction.

The premise of progress as an evolutionary context has failed. Evolution no longer coincides with progress as the Enlightenment, and in some ways also Marxism, had naively thought. In these conditions, a future subjectivity has to be thought through.

We must get used to the idea that evolution is passing through a regression, through the disintegration of the infrastructures of social civilization.

The central question that arises is the following: How can we set in motion autonomous and supportive processes of subjectivation in this regressive perspective? How can sensitivity escape the traps of depression and panic? How can sensibility maintain self-sufficient and supportive communities?

Climate change, already unfolding with all of its ferocity, is the demonstration of the irreversibility of this catastrophe. Since the chain of catastrophic automatisms has reached such a complexity that it exceeds the ability of voluntary action to understand and govern, only desertion is strategically rational and ethically acceptable: "strategically rational" in that that desertion can produce effects of change that no commitment is capable of producing, and "ethically acceptable" in that in the current conditions action implies unacceptable violence or a pact with the enemy that takes away any emancipatory power from the action itself.

Not only do I think that desertion is the only behavior that can ethically allow us to escape inhumanity, I also think it is the only strategy capable of bringing down capitalism, a system based on the mobilization of social energies. Withdrawing our energies from the social game is by no means a renunciation of struggle: it is the most radical form of class struggle imaginable; the only form that can spread widely among a generation that labels itself the "last generation." Desertion is the only form of class struggle that may have a chance of success today.

I define desertion in a broad sense, as a behavior that is not limited to abandoning the battlefield but implies disengagement from any collaboration, from any complicity, with a murderous system, and which simultaneously implies inhabiting the world in a way that is compatible with the exhaustion we are all faced with. Somewhere Deleuze wrote that when one is escaping, she is not only escaping but also looking for new weapons, new ways to survive.

Understood in this way, desertion may grow into a strategic program capable of interpreting and organizing a trend that is already inscribed in contemporary ethics, in the spontaneous depressive disposition that is spreading all over as part the psycho-deflation caused by the pandemic.

We are helplessly witnessing the private appropriation of public goods, the destruction of the social achievements of the past century, and the devastation of the environment. Now we should thoroughly accept impotence and turn it into an invincible weapon.

Desertion is an ethical choice, and a rational strategy too.

Finally, I want to clarify that I have no intention of

persuading anyone to follow my suggestions. I'm suggesting nothing — in fact, I don't mean to plead a cause. What interests me is only interpreting a tendency that I see inscribed in the spontaneous behavior of the majority of people: in the creeping depression, in the deafening silence of the world. I intend to bring out a trend that grows powerful in the depth of the collective unconscious — one of abstentionism, of absenteeism, of passivity, of desertion.

One last consideration: under the present conditions, we must remember the Stoic ethics which prescribes the imperturbability of the soul at any juncture. We also must remember Don Juan's words to Castaneda: "The important thing is not to win or lose, the important thing is to be impeccable." And we have to remember Seneca, who suggested that deserting life is the only ethical choice to be made in the face of intolerable injustice when that intolerable injustice cannot be matched and defeated. Such stoicism, however, is a choice that can only be individual, while in this book I deal mainly instead with a collective ethics.

At this level, I can only read the signs of the malady, interpret those signs as clues of hidden possibility, and help that possibility to emerge and become conscious. This is essential in order not to misunderstand what I am going to say.

Part 1

Desertion as Ethical Choice

Will, Potency, Chaos

Ethics Is the Wisdom of Action

Ethics concerns, in Greek, the search for a good "way of being,"
for a wise course of action. The wise man is he who, able to
distinguish those things which are his responsibility from those
which are not, restricts his will to the former while impassively
enduring the latter.

Alain Badiou, *Ethics: An Understanding of Evil*[1]

When we speak of ethical choice, we assume that the action
we take as the result of that ethical choice will be free, as ethics
without free will is merely a description of the conditions
under which action is taken. These conditions are the forms
of life of the community to which we belong, in which we
have formed ourselves, and are also the cultural rules that are
tacitly assumed and the economic conditions that generally
appear as inevitable constrictions. These conditions, among
many others, act as limits that shape and restrict our ability to
freely choose our acts and our place in the world. Therefore,
reasoning about ethics implies questioning freedom.

If action is rigorously determined by the conditions
in which the subject is formed, we cannot even speak of
ethical action. The idea of free will is crucial in the cultural

---

1 Alain Badiou (2001) *Ethics: An Understanding of Evil*, Verso Books, p. 19.

common ground of modernity, to the point of becoming a sort of mythical fetish, charging the word "freedom" with an exorbitant ideological value devoid of any philosophical ground.

Liberalism, the ideology that has marked the historical and economic development of late modernity, has turned freedom into an absolute value, the undetermined dimension in which the power of acting manifests itself. History and life experience, however, spell out that this political mythology is philosophically ungrounded.

In fact, there is freedom to act only within the limits of our potency. We are not free to accomplish an action that we do have not the potency to bring off. Therefore, the concept of ethics must first of all be detached from the romantic illusion of an unlimited freedom of action. At that point, having abandoned the claim of omniscience and omnipotence, we can understand why it is impossible to react to the current political and social crisis with a strengthening of the will. Only an enhancement of knowledge, a different interpretation, can open a way beyond our current crisis. Only the abandonment of the claimed supremacy of the human, only a non-hierarchical relationship with the other (nature, society), will allow us to get in tune with chaos and recognize its rhythm. It is not the faculty of will, but the faculty of sensibility, that is in question here.

The concept of free will itself emerged within the framework of humanistic culture as the independence of the human will from the will of God, but it was also intended as the efficacy of free action. These are two distinct faces of the notion of freedom: without independence, human action is only a manifestation of providence; and without political efficacy, will is just a vacuous agitation without practical consequences.

Humanistic philosophy emancipated Adam and, above all, Eve from providential prefiguration, and therefore attributed to man (and above all to woman) the faculty to choose between alternatives: original sin acquires, then, a positive value through all its consequences, namely the historical evolution of mankind.

God decided to suspend his intrusiveness so to give humans the possibility of carrying out actions that do not correspond to His law, actions that create a dimension of Being not shaped by His omnipotent will. God wanted His creatures to be independent from providence, that is, from the omnipotent omniscience of the divine will. From the beginning, therefore, free will presents itself as a scandal, a paradox.

The potency of will and the freedom of voluntary action are the conditions of the political evolution of the modern age. These two conditions, however, are not naturally given and are not intrinsic to human nature. After asserting the independence of human choice from the will of God, humanism proceeded to attribute to human will an exorbitant potency, especially when, after the Scientific Revolution, free will met the potency of knowledge, whose extension was deemed boundless. Technology, the active manifestation of knowledge and the engine for the submission of nature to the constantly expanding economy, gives man this seemingly limitless potency.

However, the power of human will only *claims* to be limitless, and so the political and philosophical foundations of Western capitalist societies are based on the unproven assumption of the omnipotence of the will. Experience has proved the illusory nature of this assumption, which has paved the way for the political rhetoric of the Western world.

Ethical choice, on the contrary, does not arise in the context of pure indetermination, as it is limited and influenced by the cultural and material conditions that circumscribe the space of possibility. This means that freedom exists in the space of potency, not the other way round: we are not free to choose whatever we want, but we are free to choose only what is imaginable within our psycho-cultural situation, and only what is in the reach of our potency.

This is the lesson of Baruch Spinoza, who puts potency at the center of the very dynamics of ethical action. Not will, but passions — the soul's affections and the modes of the mind — define the field in which ethical action can be conceived. Ethics is consciousness of action, but action is not free in an absolute sense: freedom is limited by the very conditions in which choice is conceived and made.

Therefore, ethics does not imply the unconditional freedom of will, but the historical and psychological situation that limits, or rather shapes, an ethical choice. When Max Weber speaks of protestant ethics, he refers to those religious and cultural features that make possible the formation of what he calls "the spirit of capitalism." Ethics is not the consciousness of totally free acts, but consciousness up to certain point, free of actions that are limited by their own conditions.

The conditions of ethical choice have changed in the late modern period: in the last few decades we have witnessed the magnification of technological power, followed by the increase in complexity of the technical environment. Capitalism, therefore, has taken on the features of an omnipotent and hyper-complex system, in the face of which the will of individuals, and also the will of the organized majority, counts for nothing.

This is why, as neoliberalism has untethered the dynamics of capital accumulation from collective interest, totally submitting social activity to the interests of private enterprises, the word "freedom" has lost all connection to real life, becoming a deceptive illusion. Democratic ethics thus functions as a cynical trap in which the collective will, rendered powerless, is extinguished.

In the modern era, science and politics have reduced the complexity of the world to the regularity of physical laws and the intentionality of political laws. This reduction has been indisputably effective, enabling the creation of the technical universe based on the laws of causality, determination, and predictability. But that effectiveness was linked to the particular technical conditions of modernity; that is, to the mechanical character of modern technology. As intelligent devices proliferate, cognitive and practical power is reduced due to the increase in technological complexity.

Technology has developed as a means of freeing humans from the external conditions of nature. Subsequently, it has instead become a second nature, as humans have been subjected to the algorithmic order.

The castle of classical science was built on the assumption of a recognizable and repeatable causal determination, but the regularity of mechanical laws proved unable to exhaustively explain the complexity of subatomic matter, such that the mechanical paradigm of determinist causality was partially replaced, or supplemented, with an indeterministic paradigm. Simultaneously political will became less and less effective as the environment grew more and more complex, up to the point of escaping the ability to understand and to decide.

The more complexity prevails over human understanding and political control, the more will and decision are replaced by automatisms. Science and politics are unable to master both the biological and neurological micro-processes and the catastrophic planetary macro-processes provoked by centuries of extractivism. This is why political potency has dissolved, giving way to the pathetic mental confusion and hypocritical bigotry of the political class.

Those who take advantage of the automatisms inscribed in technology and economics hide behind the fiction of democratic decision-making, but democratic decision in fact decides nothing, because the marriage of technology and economics has reduced the margin of alternatives to the point of irrelevance.

Technology and economics have together built an order that escapes political decision-making and becomes more and more complex, more and more full of automatic interdependencies, but the very complexity of this order pushes it to the limit of ungovernability and unknowability. At that point, unpredictable and apparently marginal chaotic factors can paralyze the automatic decision-making machine to the extent of revealing not only the powerlessness of politics, but also the powerlessness of technology itself, of the same automatisms.

During the Covid-19 pandemic, the virus acted as a chaotic factor that jeopardized the automatic chains of social order until technology was able to produce a vaccine that reduced its deadly effect, creating new automatic chains (sanitary discipline). In the same way, the pollution generated by social production has determined effects of chaos on the climate and on the future of the planet, phenomena that are too complex and too large to be reduced to the scope of will and reason. Some of these disruptive catastrophic processes are also irreversible and self-feeding, further emphasizing the powerlessness of political will.

The conditions revealed by the pandemic, but also by increasingly frequent environmental catastrophes, expose the impotence of political action and reveal the inadequacy of democracy in the face of the disarranging effects of unlimited growth. Technology, which in the past increased the power of organized will, has ended up building a global machine that surpasses and annihilates that power.

The helplessness we feel in the face of such ungovernable chaotic factors as the global pandemic or climate change fuels a sense of anger, frustration, humiliation, and ultimately aggressiveness. The neo-reactionary and sovereign movements that have spread all over the world in the last six years since Trump's victory in the American elections find their material root and motivation in this feeling of powerlessness and excess. The nationalist reaction aims to reaffirm the governing sovereignty of the nation, with its hierarchies of sexual and economic racial power.

Of course, the project of subjecting chaos to the traditional order of nation, ethnicity, or religion is destined to fail, but the aggressive drive is not reduced; on the contrary, it grows more and more furious. The more authoritarian governments fail in their attempts to subdue chaos, the more they accentuate their authoritarianism to the point of setting in motion processes of aggression, such as the war that Putin has launched against Ukraine and against Western hegemony as a whole.

Skeptic Ethics and Self-Love

Since the origins of the Christian era, ethics has been linked to the relationship between human will and divine power. In Augustine's thought, the will takes on a decisive role, starting the philosophical reflection on subjectivity. But in the unstable and ever-changing relationship between the margins of free will and the limits set by reality, we are led to realize that all normative ethics is founded on shaky grounds.

Only a skeptical attitude allows us to exercise a choice between alternatives in a realistic and effective way, because it attributes the function of limit to the historical, environmental, and psychological context, conditions that cannot be ignored. Moral imperatives based on absolute norms, based on the *a priori* of practical reason, are nothing but ineffective, empty affirmations, like the much vaunted and unusable formula "act as if your action were the rule of universal action."

As Wilhelm Weischedel writes:

Ethics go in search of valid and binding criteria while skepticism is itself extremely distrustful of anything that claims absolute validity. An ethics poses and affirms something, while skepticism destroys all presuppositions and does nothing but problematize. The skeptical ethical formula therefore seems to weld together two concepts that contradict each other in a radical way… ethics requires imperativity, skepticism denies it.[2]

In late modern times, faith in the universality of morals has faded, and the relativization of judgment has led to a misunderstanding. Irony has been mistaken for cynicism.

Cynicism is when our semiotic behavior bends to the force of established power. Irony does not trust any primacy and does not bend to any force, because irony knows that language is just a game whose rules are continuously changed, transgressed, and betrayed. Ethical choice therefore does not depend on any universal foundation. This is why skepticism authorizes irony as linguistic criterion of ethics.

---

2   Wilhelm Weischedel (1998) *Etica scettica*, Il Melangolo, p. 23.

Weischedel acknowledges that there is a logical contradiction between the prevailing conception of ethics as a system of imperatives and the skeptical *epoké*, which knows how to suspend judgment and how to renounce norms and imperatives. If we want to go beyond this contradiction, we should ground ethical judgment in pleasure and self-love rather than in universal norms and imperative rules.

An imperative ethics presupposes a moral authority based on institutions of totalitarian Truth (the Church, the State, the Party). Postmodern power, however, has dissolved any reference to such foundational truth, and consequently has eroded the ethical authority that imposed the respect of law. Postmodern power is instead based on the internalization of norms, promulgated by automated techno-linguistic tools (*dispositifs*). The coherence of the system is enabled by psychological automatisms that often take the form of transgressive conformism.

We cannot, therefore, ground a political ethics in universal moral values, but only in empathy, in reciprocal sympathy, in care for the other and her suffering, in pleasure, and in respect for oneself.

In conclusion, I will say that ethics can only be based on sensibility. This means that aesthetics, which is the science of sensibility, is the foundation of ethics. Ethics cannot be based on a normative or imperative foundation, but should be conceived of instead as a therapeutic act: the reactivation of empathy as a condition for pleasure. The Buddhist notion of Great Compassion is not a moral imperative, but the sensible perception of the body of the other as an extension of one's own.

Our choices do not depend on universal norms, but on a criterion that is rooted in experience. What is this criterion if not the singular sensitivity, the perception of pleasure and suffering, that our actions can produce in ourselves and in the other? A non-imperative ethics is therefore an empathic ethics based on the principle of sympathy — that is, on a common interest in pursuing the maximum pleasure for all sentient beings with whom we come directly or indirectly into contact through our actions:

> No relationship between logos and ethos, or between philosophy and politics, is conceivable if we do not go to the root of the relationship between logos and aisthesis, between theory and sensation. Only in the connection of thought with pleasure (and with pain) do ethics and politics find a not insignificant foundation.[3]

Ethics, Aesthetics, Chaosmosis

Pleasure should not be conceived of as a natural thing, independent from the cultural conditions in which sensibility is shaped. Pleasure is culturally defined, and the image of pleasure is socially constructed: media, particularly advertising, play a crucial role in the formation of the expectations of pleasure.

What is the image of pleasure that the consumerist society has shaped? What are the expectations of pleasure modeled by the media sphere?

While desire is the creation of a singular universe, the emanation of a world of possibilities, persons, bodies, and voices — attractors that induce a tension in the sensitive organism — pleasure is the reduction of the tension between the singular organism and the surrounding world, the dissolving of

---

3   Paolo Virno (2002) *Esercizi di esodo. Linguaggio e azione politica*, Ombre corte, p. 13.

the cultural film that separates my body from the body of the other and from the body of the universe. Sensibility changes over time in relation to the historical environment. Therefore, the ability to feel pleasure depends on the historical and cultural context.

The pathology induced by the semi-capitalist acceleration of the infosphere has shifted pleasure from the sphere of sensitivity to the sphere of mediation: the symbolic surrogate produced by the media spreads a viral mutation in the psychosphere. This is why the ethical question finds its place in the field of aesthetics. Aesthetics, the sphere of sensitivity, is the place for ethical policy in the semi-capitalist era.

The new generation of Internet natives and precarious workers suffers from a disorder that is essentially aesthetic. The root of revolt in the generation that animates the Fridays for Future movement has not only a moral character, it is also and above all aesthetic: it is a disgust at suffocating over-consumption, at the ugliness of rampant plastic, at the cynicism of those who have suffered long exposure to neoliberal domination, and also at the spectacle of politics.

In his book *Chaosmosis*, Félix Guattari speaks of an "aesthetic paradigm," writing that aesthetic perception reframes the political and the ethical sphere. "Aesthetics" here is meant in the etymological sense: the science of the perception of pleasure and suffering, and the trans-monadic science that investigates what enables empathy.

In Guattari's words, the aesthetic paradigm marks the beginning of "a politics and ethics of singularity, breaking with consensus, the infantile 'reassurance' distilled by dominant subjectivity."[4] There is a strong relation between aesthetic

---

4   Felix Guattari (1995) *Chaosmosis: An Ethico-Aesthetic Paradigm*, Indiana University press, p. 117.

and psychotherapeutic action, according to Guattari. The problem of the relation between chaos-inducing speed and the singularity of living temporalities is crucial.

In order to adapt to the temporal flow, the mind has to build its own temporalities, what Guattari called "*ritournelles*," that enable orientation in the world. The concept of the ritournelle ("refrain") is linked with the schizoanalytic vision: ritournelles are indeed niches of the self in which it is possible to create a singular cosmos that is able to enter into relation with the shared cosmos:

> Art is not chaos but a composition of chaos that yields the vision or sensation, so that it constitutes, as Joyce says, a chaosmos, a composed chaos — neither foreseen nor preconceived. Art transforms chaotic variability into *chaoid* variety [...] Art struggles with chaos but it does so in order to render it sensory even through the most charming character, the most enchanted landscape.[5]

By "aesthetic paradigm," Guattari refers to the central position that sensibility acquires in the present, when production and media are inscribed deeply in the sensible emanation of the world. When the syntony of organism and environment is disturbed by the acceleration of the infosphere, art records and makes visible this dissonance while simultaneously creating the conditions for the formation of new possibilities of becoming.

As a tool of schizotherapy, art acts in two different directions: as a diagnosis of the psychospheric pollution, and as a cure of the dysphoric relation between the world and the

---

5   Gilles Deleuze and Félix Guattari (1994) *What is Philosophy?*, Columbia University Press, pp. 204–5.

organism, especially of the relation among bodies in the social space.

Buddhist thinkers speak of "Great Compassion" as the capacity to feel the continuity of my body and your body and the co-respiration of ten thousand living beings. But sensibility itself is at stake in the present mutation.

The present acceleration of nervous mobilization, an effect of the growing exploitation of the social brain, endangers the sensitive ability to conjoin. This is the current pathology of pleasure.

Panic and depressive pathologies are spreading among the precarious hyper-connected generation, as Jean Twinge shows in her books on the subject.[6] Suicide, the first cause of death among young people, takes the form of aggressive actions: suicidal terrorism, mass shootings.

Forced to constantly accelerate the rhythm of the nervous reaction to info-stimuli, the precarious generation experiences the speeding up of work and hedonistic consumerism as a factory of unhappiness.

The social expression of this generation will not be, in my opinion, a political movement; it will rise up in an ethical and aesthetic insurrection, a movement for the recomposition and re-conjunction of the collective body beyond connectivity, a new ethics based on irony.

Skepticism, Cynicism, Irony

Since we left the realm of metaphysics, skepticism has become our condition of knowledge. Therefore, skepticism must also

---

6   Jean Twenge (2017) *iGen: Why Today's Super-Connected Kids Are Growing Up Less Rebellious, More Tolerant, Less Happy — and Completely Unprepared for Adulthood — and What That Means for the Rest of Us*, Atria Books.

be the starting point for ethics and politics, if moralism and totalitarianism are to be avoided.

Pyrrho of Elis was a Greek philosopher known for first formulating the skeptical claim. Like Socrates, Pyrrho left us no texts, but we do know that he lived at the turn of the fourth century BC and participated in the expedition to India, following Alexander. Diogenes Laërtius tells that he was first a painter, then heard the lessons of Brisone, and later had contact with the Gymnosophists in India. What we know of his doctrine and of his teaching comes to us from Timon, who allows us to see Pyrrho as the precursor to Sextus Empiricus, Saturninus, and others who lived in the Hellenistic period who defined themselves as skeptics.

In its original Pyrrhonic version, skepticism is the philosophical effect of exposure to the thought of otherness. Pyrrho's thought was nurtured by the discovery that Greek knowledge was relative, unlike the knowledge claims of the Persians of the Indians, particularly those of the gymnosophists — the sages who based knowledge on corporeality — whose thought and practices he was exposed to.

Thanks to Pyrrho, Greek ethical thought became open to sapiential alterity, making possible the "*skepsis*" — the suspension of judgment (*epoké*) at the gnoseological level, and impeccability (*apazeia*) at the moral level.[7] The experience of otherness suggested to Pyrrho a suspension of belief.

Since modern philosophy has emancipated itself from the metaphysical regime of belief, we have also discovered, with Mallarmé and Heisenberg, that poetic and even scientific language does not represent the world, but instead creates a world in the space of uncertainty. An unintended effect of

---

7   "*Apazeia*" is often translated as "apathy," but I prefer the translation "impeccability."

this emancipation of language from the metaphysical regime of belief was a misunderstood identification of cynicism and irony.

Cynicism and irony are rhetorical forms and ethical attitudes founded on the suspension of belief in a fixed relationship between reality and language. But the distance and opposition between of cynicism and irony are, from my point of view, more important than their similarity.

Cynicism is a form of enunciation in a regime of disbelief, in which enunciation (the act of subjectivation) is a way of obtaining or maintaining power, or at least a way of obtaining something in complicity with the established reality.

In the shadow of neoliberal dogma, cynicism is the only accepted language, the only cool behavior. In *Critique of Cynical Reason*, published in 1983, Peter Sloterdijk argues that cynicism is the dominant mental model of the era following the last utopia (in 1968). Sloterdijk does not describe the cynic as an exceptional character, but as the average man — this is the difference between modern cynicism and the ancient philosophical position of Diogenes. While Diogenes and his cynic followers were ascetic individualists who rejected acquiescence to the order of power, modern cynics are a massive population of conformists who know very well that the law of power is bad, but who are willing to bend to it because they think nothing else can be done.

Irony begins at the same skeptical starting point, but goes in a totally different direction. Of course, ironic language can be an expression of cynicism, but irony and cynicism are totally dissimilar from an ethical point of view, and irony (not moralism) is the aesthetic critique of the prevailing cynicism of power and servility.

Vladimir Jankélévitch defines cynicism as "disappointed moralism" — a judgment based on a fixed system of moral values which, however, modifies its intention. The cynic is someone who has believed in the truth and who has lost his faith. The ironic discourse never presupposes the existence of a truth that must be fulfilled or realized. Irony presupposes the infinite nature of the interpretative process, while cynicism presupposes a lost faith. Having lost his faith, the cynic yields to power, a substitute for truth, while the ironic does not need any truth, because pleasure and sensitivity are the only source of truth.Irony presupposes a relationship of complicity and solidarity between participants in the dialogic process. In the words of Jankélévitch, "Irony is not disenchanted for the good reason that it has never accepted to be enchanted."[8]

The common starting point of irony and cynicism is this: both the cynic and the ironic suspend their belief in the moral content of truth. They know that truth and good do not exist in the mind of God or in history, and they know that human behavior is not based on respect for any law, but on empathy, shared pleasure, and great compassion.

The cynic bends to the law while laughing at its values as false and hypocritical, while the ironic escapes the law to create a linguistic space in which the law has no effect. The cynic is the one who wants to be on the side of power, but does not believe in its moral correctness. The ironic simply refuses the game, recreating the world as an effect of linguistic enunciation.

Meaning is only the effect of the interpretation of cultural flows running through the social space, changing language, expectations, and forms of self-representation. Autonomous

---

8   Vladimir Jankélévitch (2011) *L'ironie*, Flammarion, p. 32.

creative movement got rid of the idea that the horizon is marked by historical necessity and experimented with the ironic form of political action.

In the space of moral uncertainty, enunciation and action are devoid of any ontological foundation. Neither God nor history guarantees the final triumph of truth, and in the same way, neither guarantees the relationship between signified and signifier. This is the common ground of irony and cynicism. Irony and cynicism are opposed: irony suspends the meaning of the signifier and freely chooses between many different possible interpretations; cynicism starts from the same suspension, but narrows the space of interpretation, thinking that only what is powerful, efficient, and victorious is good.

The ironic sleeps well because no one can wake her from her dreams. The cynic is a light sleeper, because she sleeps without dreaming, and wakes up as soon as power calls her.

Experience, Sympathy, Subjectivity

"Democracy" is the most cherished value of modern, liberal political discourse, but it has been emptied of meaning as economic power has used it as a way to legitimize itself, particularly in the second half of the twentieth century.

Democracy comes in different forms: liberal democracy, popular democracy, sovereign democracy, and so on. But the Anglo-American world has attributed to itself a monopoly on democracy such that any other interpretation of the concept must be rejected and reformed. The liberal meaning of democracy is accompanied by a universalistic claim that transforms it into a political imperative, a model from which no one can escape.

It is therefore liberal universalism that we must deal with, and to do so I refer to Immanuel Kant, the main advocate of the universalism of Reason. I do not intend to scrutinize the cultural and political consequences produced by liberal ideology. Rather, I am interested in examining the philosophical premises of political universalism, and to do so we must engage with some passages from Kant's *Critique of Practical Reason*.

The "practical reason" that Kant is talking about wants to be as universal as pure reason. When Kant proposes to act "in such a way that the maxim of your will can always be valid as the principle of a universal legislation,"[1] he disregards the conditions in which an action unfolds and chooses to ignore the singularity and uniqueness of these conditions. According to him, in fact, "the pure will, which is free, finds itself in a sphere that is totally different from the empirical sphere."[2] Consequently, there is at most no relation, and possibly even a relation of opposition, between the moral norm and the pleasure or suffering of beings: "The principle of one's happiness is the total opposite of the principle of morality."[3] The practical reason theorized by Kant is not conditioned by circumstances or by events, but is "unconditional reason," which in its absolute freedom establishes the rules of behavior.

Precisely for this reason, Kant's practical reason is not very useful in our present situation, where every day we make choices based on our interest and pleasure. The goal of ethical policy is to make the pleasure of ten thousand beings coincide, to create a harmony of interests, not to disregard those interests and that quest for pleasure.

Modern political thought has tried to achieve this convergence and harmony in different ways. Liberalism conceives of an invisible hand of the market which redistributes prosperity; socialism conceives of a strong state will, capable of imposing equality. But as we know, these attempts have not achieved their purpose, and we are now obliged to reflect on the consequences of the collapse of these two models.

For Kant, man is a moral subject able to act with free will, but the history and conditions of our time show that the human will is less and less free and less and less efficient, as its potency is limited by economic and technical automatisms.

---

1 Immanuel Kant, *Critique of Practical Reason*, Part 1, §7.

2 *Ibid.*, Part 1, note 1.

3 *Ibid.*, Part 1, note 2.

The universality of the Kantian rule is based on the universal character that Reason attributes to itself, but when we deal with existence, Reason loses the ability to understand and therefore to act.

Kant writes that the universality of moral law is substantial as long as the will is not dependent on pathological conditions: "These laws lack that necessity which, if it is to be practical, must necessarily be independent of pathological conditions and therefore accidentally attached to the will."[4] The problem is that what are defined here as "pathological conditions" are not an exceptional form of distortion of the will, but the real, concrete form in which the will manifests itself. Existence, in a certain sense, is nothing else than a pathology of Reason: individual existence, and *a fortiori* collective existence, is interwoven with that pathology.

Kant himself actually adds that the moral rule is valid objectively and universally only when we ignore the singularity of the conditions in which the subject acts:

> A legislation of reason must merely presuppose itself, because the rule is objective and universally valid only when it is in force [*gilt*] without those subjective, accidental conditions which distinguish one rational entity from another.[5]

The conceptual construction at the center of Kant's philosophy, which can be summarized by the expression "*Ich denke*," is aimed at assembling the universal conditions of the functioning of the human mind, but ignores (consciously

---

4   *Ibid*, Part 1, Chapter, 1.
5   *Ibid.*

and expressly) existential singularity in its psychological and cultural specificity. Therefore, this concept (whose influence has been enormous in the philosophical landscape of late modernity) is unable to capture the core of the activity of thinking; that is, contingency, or, in a sense, the pathological.

The contingent circumstances in which mental activity happens are described by psychology, anthropology, and sociology, but according to Kant, ethical thinking must only deal with the *a priori* categories of the moral law

Ich denke, "I think." The subject of the sentence ("I") has forgotten they have a body. Actually, Kant regards the body as inessential to the perspective of knowledge, as transcendental apperception is independent of any experience, and therefore practical reason expresses its ethical imperative within *a priori* conditions. These conditions are universal because they are exempt from the mark of experience, which is eminently singular.

The Kantian moral law has to do with forms of will: it does not deal with what we actually want within the concrete conditions of existence, but instead refers to the legitimacy of wishing what we wish, of doing what we actually do. In order to distance himself from empiricism and utilitarianism, Kant installs formalism at the center of his ethical scene. But this gigantic effort to found a universalist morality reveals its own paucity as soon as we compare it to the historical reality of Western modernity, which wants to be Kantian and founds the universalistic claim of liberal democracy on the premises of Kantian formalism.

The greatness of Immanuel Kant certainly consists in having conceived of knowledge and experience itself within the *a priori* coordinates of transcendental apperception, that is, in having founded the activity of perceiving and knowing on the constitution of the subject of knowledge, which precedes knowledge and perception itself, allowing him to divine the forms that make knowledge and perception possible, regardless of the contents they elaborate. These forms are transcendental in the sense that they are independent of experience, but experience is only possible within the scope of these forms.

"I think" is therefore a function that makes possible the relationship between thinker and thought, but the thinker does not appear there. The thinker as a sentient, emotional, historically situated organism does not appear in Kantian discourse.

Experience and Subjectivation

In his 1953 book *Empiricism and Subjectivity*, Gilles Deleuze writes on *A Treatise of Human Nature* by David Hume. According to his non-polemical argument, Deleuze reads Hume's as a special form of empiricism, opposed to the Kantian variant, in order to establish the foundations of ethics and simultaneously to propose a theory of subjectivation that is somehow divergent from the concept of identity:

> Hume's project entails the *substitution of a psychology of the mind by a psychology of the mind's affections.* The constitution of a psychology of the mind is not at all possible, since this psychology cannot find in its object the required constancy or universality; only a psychology of affections will be capable of constituting the true science of humanity.[6]

---

6   Gilles Deleuze (2001) *Empiricism and Subjectivity: An Essay on Hume's Theory of Human Nature*, Columbia University Press, p. 21.

Deleuze reads *A Treatise of Human Nature* as relating an empiricism of lived experience, which is different from an empiricism of the thing. What interests Hume, and Deleuze too, is placing the foundation of knowledge on the ground of experience, intended as an event of subjectivity, not the empiricity of the thing that gives itself as an object of experience. Here is exposed the genesis of the Deleuzean thought: from Hume to Bergson, the concept of experience is linked with the concept of subjectivity. "Ideas," writes Deleuze, referring to Hume's text, "are connected in the mind — not by the mind."[7]

Ideas get together and conjoin in the mind, and this association is the mind itself; the conjunction of objects of imagination gives way to the becoming thought. These assertions are key to Deleuze's anti-Kantian stance, which is also anti-formalist and anti-structuralist. This is important for this book's argument, especially in terms of its ethical implications. Aiming to ground an ethics of duty, Kant criticized Hume because he did not establish ethical choice on the foundation of an absolute norm, but on the experience of pleasure and practicality. On the contrary, Kant wants to oppose ethical reason to the experience of pleasure, and considers aesthetics as the middle ground (*Mittleglied*) between pure reason and practical reason: "The aesthetic pleasure that is based on the gratification of the inclinations can never be appropriate."[8]

Kant has de-substantialized the Cartesian "cogito" and transformed the act of thought into a mere abstract faculty of thinking, but his *a priori* establishes everything and explains nothing, because what we learn from lived experience is that there are no morals, only anthropology, psychology, and most

---

7   *Ibid.*, p. 5.
8   Kant, *Critique of Practical Reason*, Part 2, Chapter 2.

of all aesthetics. If we want to establish the ground of ethical judgment on something other than the abstract, bodiless thought of Kant, we must refer to the environment in which the subject lives, to the cultural coordinates of her orientation, to her psychology, and most of all to the attraction and repulsion that the subject perceives, to the sentiment of suffering and pleasure.

"I never can catch myself at any time without a perception, and never can observe any thing but the perception," writes Hume.

> But setting aside some metaphysicians of this kind, I may venture to affirm of the rest of mankind, that they are nothing but a bundle or collection of different perceptions, which succeed each other with an inconceivable rapidity, and are in a perpetual flux and movement. [...] The mind is a kind of theatre, where several perceptions successively make their appearance; pass, re-pass, glide away, and mingle in an infinite variety of postures and situations. [...] They are the successive perceptions only, that constitute the mind; nor have we the most distant notion of the place, where these scenes are represented, or of the materials, of which it is compos'd.[9]

Having made these his premises, Hume wonders how the continuity of the experience that is perceived as identity (or "being oneself") can arise. To this question, Hume offers an answer that seems to me most useful for dissolving the fog that surrounds the notion of identity.

Identity and diversity, he writes, are the same thing considered from two distinct points of view — what we take

---

9   David Hume (1956) *Treatise of Human Nature*, Everyman Library, p. 239.

for an invariable subject (identical to itself) is in fact a flow of ever-different self-perceptions:

> Thus the controversy concerning identity is not merely a dispute of words. For when we attribute identity, in an improper sense, to variable or interrupted objects, our mistake is not confin'd to the expression, but is commonly attended with a fiction, either of something invariable and uninterrupted, or of something mysterious and inexplicable, or at least with a propensity to such fictions.[10]

The soul, or the substance of which the subject is composed, at this point dissolves and is replaced by experience reflecting on itself and a projection that in some cases we tend to fix as identity.

In fact, adds Hume, the fixation of identity conceals or distorts the singularization that the gaze of others projects on us. It's not identity but becoming other that makes it possible to understand the world and founds the ethical intention of acting.

> In general we may remark, that the minds of men are mirrors to one another, not only because they reflect each other's emotions, but also because those rays of passions, sentiments and opinions may be often reverberated, and may decay away by insensible degrees.[11]

This phenomenological conception of self-perception allows Hume to define virtue as the faculty of producing pleasure (in oneself and the other), and vice as the faculty of causing

---

10 *Ibid.*, p. 241.

11 *Ibid.*, p. 243.

pain to oneself and to the other. In this way, as Deleuze explains, Hume makes it possible to state what subjectivity is: "The subject is not a quality but rather the qualification of a collection of ideas. [...] It is a governing principle, a schema, a rule of construction."[12]

The subject is nothing but the singular style that makes possible the creation of a singular universe of meaning. The subject is the effect of a strategy of survival, self-affirmation, and pleasure, a strategy pursued by a conscious organism whose existence cannot be reduced to anything else:

> The subject is the entity which, under the influence of the principle of utility, pursues a goal or an intention; it organizes means in view of an end and, under the influence of the principles of association, establishes relations among ideas. Thus, the collection becomes a system. The collection of perceptions, when organized and bound, becomes a system.[13]

The subject is the rule of construction of the overall meaning of perceptual associations; it is the dynamic systematization of a collection of experiences, organized according to the pursuit of a goal, an intention:

> The subject is defined by the movement through which it is developed. Subject is that which develops itself. [...] Such is the dual power of subjectivity: to believe and to invent, to assume the secret powers and to presuppose abstract or distinct powers. In these two senses, the subject is normative; it creates norms or general rules.[14]

---

12 Deleuze, *Empiricism and Subjectivity*, p. 64.
13 *Ibid.*, p. 98.
14 *Ibid.*, pp. 85–6.

The world is the dynamic intersection point of flows of imagination that proceed from countless minds. Ontology is thus dissolved into an infinite game of mirrors, and the event is the deploying of experience before and outside any conceptualization. This psychodynamic integration is made possible by what Hume names "sympathy."

Let's go back to the above quote: "In general we may remark, that the minds of men are mirrors to one another." Recent research in the field of neuroscience confirm Hume's intuition: Vittorio Gallese speaks in fact of "mirror neurons" when referring to the ability of the human brain to reflect the emotion of the other and to interact with this emotion in a consistent way.[15] This consistency depends on our brain's ability to mimic and consequently to interpret the meaning of the intentional signs sent by another brain.

We must start from experience, because, as Deleuze says,

> we must begin with *this* experience because it is *the* experience. It does not presuppose anything else and nothing else precedes it. It is not the affection of an implicated subject, nor the modification or mode of a substance.[16]

It is experience that produces the content that makes up the mind. And the mind is nothing but the self-reflective evolution of the experience of a body animated by intelligence.

Deleuze concludes his book on Hume's *Treatise* with the following words:

---

15 Vittorio Gallese, "Mirror Neurons and the Social Nature of Language: The Neural Exploitation Hypothesis," *Social Neuroscience*, 2008; 3(3–4): 317–33. doi: 10.1080/17470910701563608.

16 *Ibid.*, p. 88.

Philosophy must constitute itself as the theory of what we are doing, not as a theory of what there is. What we do has its principles; and being can only be grasped as the object of a synthetic relation with the very principles of what we do.[17]

Understanding Un-Reason

Let's go back to the historical context in which my meditation began — the war in Ukraine. In following the lead-up to the initial invasion and the catastrophic events that have followed, we can easily understand that Kant's universalism of Reason is of little help.

In the name of universalism, the Atlantic forces (the self-appointed free world of liberal democracies) have created conditions of isolation and humiliation for populations that are refractory to that kind of abstract universalism. Nothing is more hypocritical than liberal universalism, because the principles of freedom and human rights are only valuable for those who enjoy the required class privilege or race supremacy. The political reality is that the so-called free world uses universalism to protect its own particular interests, and it wields the universal criterion of human rights as an instrument of aggression against those who threaten the interests of the dominators. Threat, aggression, and violence are justified in the name of a universalistic philosophy that imperialists have systematically violated and used for the purposes of systemic violation.

On the other hand, there is little point in affirming the universal value of peace, which the (few) well-intentioned heirs of the pacifist movement are declaring today in order to counter the nationalist and militarist wave that is engulfing the planet. No universal principle is effective if there is no

17 *Ibid.*, p. 133.

force capable of imposing it, and the use of force contradicts precisely the universal principle that the well-intentioned would like to affirm.

If we take Hume's sympathy as an ethical criterion, the panorama becomes more interesting, albeit infinitely complex.

If we want to understand what makes contemporary experience so painful and perhaps desperate, we have to understand what pathologies we are going through, what is distorting our perception of the other and of ourselves: after decades of preaching the competitive economic war of all against all, it is normal for people to be ready for armed competition. War is no more than the continuation of politics, as Clausewitz said. In the twenty-first century, war is rather the continuation of the economic war that neoliberalism has preached and imposed worldwide.

In this context, it becomes possible to understand the "reasons" of the Russian aggressor in the historical context of his prolonged humiliation and fear of encirclement, and it also becomes possible to understand the "reasons" of the Ukrainians, who have suffered for a century under the violence and humiliation of Russian imperialism.

In this light — which is one of sympathy, its affections, and its pathologies — we can finally understand the nationalistic obsession, the vaguely insane patriotism of both sides, and the pathologies of the geopolitical relationship, but also, and more profoundly, of the emotional and social relationships at play.

Introduction to Ferocity

On the basis of the considerations put forward in this chapter, and on the basis of my definition of ethical action as action aimed at maximizing the pleasure of the universe and minimizing its suffering, I can only conclude that, with the victory of the Nazi-liberal two-headed monster in countries across the world, we have entered an era defined by the gap between historical process and ethical action. Ethical action can no longer belong to history; it is only is possible in "Her-story," a non-historical space that is characterized by a temporary suspension of the natural law. Historical action cannot be ethically motivated: it must be fierce and ferocious.

Ferocity, therefore, becomes the essential character of human history. But in reality, and on closer inspection, from the beginning of the human story it has always been so. Ferocity, from the Latin "*ferus*," indicates the savage and ultimately natural character of the intrinsic ruthlessness of action in conditions wherein the subject is stripped of the ethical qualms imposed by civilization and allowed to regress to the pre-humanized (pre-cultural) state.

It is clear that we are now living in an era of ferocity, when the relationship between humans takes place on the edge of a cliff — that is, in conditions of terror. Nazism was certainly the manifestation of programmatically declared ferocity, but in reality the entirety of modern history has been crossed by flows of ferocity that have made possible the subjugation of the colonized territories, the impoverishment of entire populations, the processes of privatization from enclosures onwards, and the general ferocity of capitalist civilization.

In the modern age, however, a counter-process has taken place that combines this ferocity with the project of humanization. Christianity affirms love as compassion, or rather the possibility of an emotional sharing that renounces oppression and ferocity by affirming closeness in Christ. In the wake of the Augustinian variant of Christianity, Humanism affirms the possibility of the independence of human law from the law of Nature.

Then the Enlightenment developed the idea of human law as an expression of a Reason that distances itself from feral nature and as a suspension of natural ferocity. Finally, socialism offered a realistic perspective on the transformation of the relations of production and exchange based on solidarity rather than on the ferocious struggle for survival.

My thinking and emotional disposition have been shaped in the wake of this cultural evolution. As such, my personal experience, like the experience of my generation, has involved precisely the decades in which the Christian, humanistic, and socialist promise seemed poised to become the ruling order of the world.

1968 can be viewed as the moment when the fulfilment of the promise of humanization seemed to be at hand, as intellectual labor emerged as the subject of social production, together with an industrial worker class that united with students in a common movement. The global transformation brought about by the events of 1968 lasted for a couple of decades, projecting on human history the prospect of social solidarity and the suspension of the law of ferocity.

On 11 September 1973, when the fascist forces of General Pinochet overthrew the democratically elected socialist government of Salvador Allende with the backing of many Western liberal democracies, this was the moment that promise was broken. Nazism returned to the scene with all of its anti-human ferocity and introduced the automatic logic of economic Nazism, oxymoronically called "liberalism."

Since then, a struggle has been waged for the defense of the human against the advance of Nazi-liberalism. That struggle has been blind because we failed to understand (until very late) that our struggle was one against Nature, against the inherent ferocity of the naturalness of the human animal, and that the ethical promise of modernity was a wager on the indefinite suspension of the natural ferocity of human history. We are now forced by the sheer weight of current events to recognize that the rule of Pinochet and Thatcher is irreversible and is leading to the giant holocaust that is already unfolding before our very eyes. At the same time, we are forced to recognize that only outside of this human history is ethical action possible.

The Psycho-Cultural Roots of the Contemporary Ethical Catastrophe

A Viral Mutation of Sensuousness and Affectivity

What are the psychological, social, and anthropological implications of the mutation that the Covid-19 pandemic has generated, or perhaps rather accelerated? Before the pandemic occurred, the conditions for an affective catastrophe were already visible as the techno-communicative conditions of connective digitization expanded.

The existential experience we all lived through during the years of the pandemic, and particularly the affective experience of the generation that was born at the turn of the millennium, caused a trauma destined to act not only on present behaviors, but above all on sensitivity and on the unconscious to come. Trauma affects empathy, and particularly erotic sensitivity, and we cannot predict what kind of adaptive change is destined to manifest itself, because trauma sets in motion ambiguous mutations: fear, avoidance of contact, and phobic sensitization to the skin of the other, but also new forms of expression of desire.

It is in the sphere of desire that the forces animating the social sphere are born and set up. Since desire is the strongest attraction, and since it is the foundation of the most radical complicity, the processes of historical subjectivation are driven by desire. But the explosion of the unconscious in the era of global connection has provoked a nervous breakdown of collective energy and triggered the pathological panic/depression cycle.

The whole discourse of love that runs through modernity, from the courtship culture of the late Middle Ages, to the matrimonial regulation of sexuality, to romantic idealization, up to the cultures of erotic transgression and sexual freedom, seems today to be reaching a turning point: perhaps it will be a pathogenic involution, or perhaps we will discover unexpected dimensions of desire. Desertion from war, and more generally from aggressive investments of desire, is the only evolutionary prospect in which this evolution can be sought. Pandemic trauma does not manifest itself immediately, but slowly works in the sphere of the unconscious; at first it acted as psycho-deflation, slowing down the pace of daily life. At the same time, however, it fully mobilized remote communication technology, increasing the social mind's dependence on the screen and digital, contactless hyper-stimulation.

Upon exiting the pandemic threshold, the social imagination has been invaded by a frenzy of violence in every aspect of contemporary existence, from geopolitics to everyday life. The pandemic has not changed the direction of the trends that were already being made manifest by decades of neoliberal globalization and connective digital technology; instead, it has accelerated them towards their full unfolding.

Social distancing has been a constant trend in the years of connectivity: the loneliness of the lockdown has reinforced this trend to the point of making it the new normal.

The experience of trauma is destined to leave an imprint on sensuality that will go far beyond the actively contagious phase, generating forms of phobic awareness.

The imperative of the social super-ego could change direction.

In the Freudian view, the imperative of the super-ego requires a renunciation of the drive (*Trieb*) and of the pleasure that comes from immediate satisfaction. On the contrary, the neoliberal imperative is aimed at arousing and mobilizing collective desire, at celebrating enjoyment and competitive aggression. It invites the pursuit of a joy that escapes continually, so stimulating competitive frenzy and frustration.

What now?

The super-ego that is emerging after the pandemic is based on responsibility and caution. What is the meaning of responsibility in the sphere of eroticism and pleasure? Should we avoid desire, should w internalize guilt?

This condition, in which erotic emotion grows dangerous and problematic, may lead to an epidemic of autism and depression, and may contribute to the accumulation of aggressive energy. Autism and emotional atrophy— a disorder of bodily perception, and particularly of the other's emotions — may become the dominant feature of the affective scape. As Wilhelm Reich states:

> The suppression of natural sexual gratification leads to various kinds of substitute gratifications. Natural aggression, for example, becomes brutal sadism which then is an essential mass-psychological factor in imperialistic wars.[1]

However, Reich's explication of the genesis of mass fascism has lost much of its pertinence since the 1960s, when mass culture was overwhelmed by waves of sexual

---

1   Wilhelm Reich (1946) *The Mass Psychology of Fascism: Ideology as Material Power*, Orgone Press, p. 16.

liberation and libertarian culture. After this period, sexual liberation was transformed by media hyper-stimulation into a phenomenon of consumerism and conformism, into the ceaseless chasing of a promised but often unreachable phantom of pleasure.

Now, past the pandemic threshold, various factors of distancing make contact less frequent, hesitant, and neurotic.

In the 1980s, AIDS produced a fear effect in the sexually transgressive landscape of the time: an interference caused by the HIV retrovirus in the erotic imagination set in motion a shift in sexual energy that in the following decade paved the way for the pornographic scene of connective eroticism.

From an aesthetic and cultural point of view, AIDS inaugurated the transition to the anthropology of virtual connection: connectivity separated desire from pleasure and established a cycle of excitement detached from the pleasure of physical conjunction.

Today, we are going through a process of psycho-mutation whose outcome may be similar to the scenario that followed the trauma of World War I.

In the time of Wilhelm Reich, fascism could be read as an effect of the repressive compression of sexual energies, but later, for Deleuze and Guattari in the 1960s, a psychotic acceleration of desiring flows paved the way for the explosion and externalization of the unconscious. Today we are facing a return of the psychic compression of which Reich spoke, but this compression has a very different genesis. It is no longer an effect of the *eruption* of psychic energies that cannot express themselves, but an *exhaustion* of those energies, a painful decline of the potency of desire. Nationalism, racism, and war are today to be seen as an *Ersatz* of stimulation, as a new kind of mass psychosis fueled by the panic of an organism that is on the verge of collapse.

For a Materialistic Foundation of the Ethical Judgment

I began by stating that ethics is the consciousness of action, and now I affirm that ethically motivated action aims to provide the maximum possible pleasure for oneself and for the surrounding universe. But it should be added that the motivation for ethical action can only be self-pleasure; "self-love," to use an expression of Fernando Savater's.

Self-love does not at all imply at selfishness as opposed to the love of the other. On the contrary, self-love must be understood as taking pleasure in the other's pleasure, as an extension and continuation of the self. As Savater writes: "It can be shown that only starting from the most elementary selfishness we can express solidarity or altruism."[2]

In the real world of social existence, this harmony based on self-love is not a given, as we know. But the counter-position of self-love and love for the other is a consequence of a distortion, as Erich Fromm suggests in *Ethics and Psychoanalysis*, where he writes that the failure of modern culture is not an effect of individualism or of the idea that it is morally good to pursue one's own interest, but is rather an effect of the distortion of the meaning of one's own interest. The problem is not that people care only about their own interest, but that they do not think properly about their own interest. The problem is not that we are too selfish; the problem is that we don't love ourselves enough. The distortion that Fromm is talking about here is the effect of the conflict between interests and between passions.

---

2 I'm translating Savater's "amor proprio" here as "self-love." Fernando Savater (1988) *Etica como amor propio*, Editorial Ariel, p. 19.

For example, a scarcity of resources requires hoarding and therefore hostility towards competitors. The rivalry of love for the "possession" of the object of desire in conditions of emotional competition can generate hatred for the competitor, who aspires to "possession" of the same "object."

Capitalism is born from the production of scarcity even where it has not existed previously, transforming every form of social relationship into competition. Only scarcity and need could force human beings to turn into salaried workers. Therefore, under capitalism, one's relationship with the other is presented as systematic hostility towards the other, and the desire of the other turns into a source of aggressive jealousy within a culture that establishes the proprietary character of the emotional relationship, a culture based on monogamous marriage and the private ownership of women.

Anyone who has experienced pleasure knows that the environment in which we live (the physical, social, psychological, relational environment) has a decisive influence on our ability to do so. For example, we know it is difficult to be happy and experience pleasure if around us there is destruction, misery, hunger, pain, and humiliation.

Impassively maintaining the quiet of the soul even in the most dramatic environmental conditions is a stoic suggestion we would like to stick to, but a collective ethical project cannot be grounded on such impeccability. Under certain environmental conditions, there is no possibility of escaping the intolerable except by removing our conscious organism from existence.

In its terminal phase (neoliberalism and financialization), capitalism has imposed on us conditions under which friendship is less and less possible, under which we are more and more often obliged to experience a divergence, an irreconcilability of collective destiny, and in which we can often only see a singular line of escape. The pursuit of profit, which necessarily involves the exploitation of the other, can only sterilize and pervert one's own pleasure, contrasting it with the pleasure of the other.

The separation of *Eros* from *Ethos*, of pleasure from duty, implicit in Kantian idealism, is peculiar to a social form in which pleasure involves a violation of the duty to produce, to accumulate. Under the conditions of capitalism, the future is identified with the endless procrastination of desire. The Protestant ethic of which Weber speaks sanctifies this renunciation of the present for the sake of a future of economic expansion.

Expansion was possible in the modern era thanks to this exchange of actual enjoyment for accumulation. That is what happened, and now we must reflect on the conclusion of this giant cycle that we have called modernity, or more precisely, capitalism.

The current exhaustion of this cycle essentially depends on the exhaustion of the energies that made this expansion possible in the first place. Can society get out of the sphere of expansion without losing the ability to produce what is necessary for survival? Or do the cultural expectations produced by capitalist consumerism make survival without expansion unthinkable, and therefore make self-destruction inevitable?

Scarcity has been and continues to be a condition of capitalist expansion. It remains a product of the expansionist culture, but expansion is no longer possible except at the cost of destruction. We are therefore living in conditions of barbarism; that is, conditions of the progressive disintegration of social civilization and civil coexistence.

A hundred thousand times in the last century we have said that our choice is either socialism or barbarism. We have been unable to create the conditions for socialism, and therefore now we must prepare ourselves for barbarism, without ceasing to look for lines of escape from looming catastrophe.

What I call barbarism is the disintegration of social civilization.

Barbarism is the ethical catastrophe we are experiencing. What is the line of flight, if not desertion?

Why War?

All war propaganda consists, in the last resort, in substituting diabolical abstractions for human beings. Similarly, those who defend war have invented a pleasant sounding vocabulary of abstractions in which to describe the process of mass murder.

Aldous Huxley, "Pacifism and Philosophy"[1]

Two Different Explanations of Human Bellicosity

Monotheism opposed eroticism and ethics, and this opposition laid the blame for unethical behavior, for sin, for ethical evil, on pleasure and promoted the economic reinvestment of the energies subtracted from it. A consequence of this was the practical and epistemic dominance of the economy over all forms of life, and the subordination of the social contract to the logic of debt, competition, and guilt.

This culpabilization and repression of libidinal energies of the collective body configures the framework that Freud describes in the *Civilization and its Discontents*, and from which Wilhelm Reich draws his theory of the genesis of fascism as the effect of compression of libidinal flows:

Under the influence of politicos, the masses blame the powers that be for wars. In the first world war it was the munition magnates, in the second the Psychopath General. This is

---

1   Aldous Huxley (1994) "Pacifism and Philosophy," Pledge Peace Union.

shifting the responsibility. The blame for the war belongs only and alone to the same masses of people who have all the means of preventing wars. The same masses of people who — partly through indolent passivity, partly through their active behavior — make possible the catastrophes from which they themselves suffer most horribly. To emphasize this fault of the masses, to give them the full responsibility, means taking them seriously. On the other hand, to pity the masses as a poor victim means treating them like a helpless child. The first is the attitude of the genuine fighter for freedom, the latter is the attitude of the politico.[2]

War could be averted if people were conscious and active, Reich says. But why are they not? Why do they allow something to happen which makes their own life hell and worsens their conditions beyond repair? Reich replies that:

In the process of killing his genital function, man has become biologically rigid. He has armored himself against that which is natural and spontaneous within him, he has lost contact with the biological function of self-regulation and is filled with a strong fear of that which is alive and free.[3]

Reich's discourse is based on the assumption of a human nature that is fundamentally harmonious when founded on the full deployment of the natural orgasmic potential of the human body. Particularly interesting is the idea that the repression of a natural drive produces an effect of muscular and psychic

---

2   Reich, *The Mass Psychology of Fascism*, p. 89.
3   *Ibid.*, p. 88.

stiffening, the creation of character armor intended to contain, divert, or suppress that drive.

We can reconnect this Reichian explanation of fascism and war with the explanation offered by the workers' and anti-militarist movements, linking war to the economic conflict between national powers, large national and global companies, financial pressure groups, and so on. These two explanations are by no means incompatible; on the contrary, they complement each other perfectly, as Reich himself knew. On the one hand, economic competition pushes groups (national, economic, military, religious) towards armed conflict. But this pressure would not be enough to force the population to undergo the immense suffering of war were it not for the psychological and political complicity of the majority, or of a certain portion of the population. Political and psychoanalytic anti-militarism therefore converge on a decisive point: war is an abnormal phenomenon, a profound distortion of social coexistence.

Marxism does not reject conflict — Marx and Engels write at the beginning of *The Communist Manifesto* that "the history of all hitherto existing society is the history of class struggles." But the class struggle must be distinguished from war, and the concept of struggle does not necessarily imply violence, the oppression of the other, or his humiliation. War is instead an unnatural phenomenon that breaks the conflictual but peaceful continuity of social coexistence. But are we sure that war is an exceptional phenomenon, a violation of the norm of inter-human relations?

In *A Terrible Love of War*, James Hillman puts forward the thesis that war, far from being an abnormal state, is the normal condition of human relations, the natural condition of the collective unconscious, in a precisely Jungian sense:

the force of mythical belonging models natural behavior in the form of war.[4] Peaceful coexistence, therefore, can only be considered as a *suspension* of this instinct, as the product of the transformation that the educational action (*Bildung*) exerts on the naturalness of the warlike instinct.

In the context of this conception, which to a certain extent I share, peace is by no means the original condition of community life, but is the effect of a cultural movement that shapes social life, regulating affective and material trades. Social civilization, which emerged in the second half of the twentieth century, is by no means a guaranteed and irreversible condition; it is instead a fragile construction, a balance of interests and passions governed by non-violent conflict and dialogue (and irony).

With the outbreak of war in Ukraine on 24 February 2022, it was announced that social civilization is disintegrating: Putin's violence is tearing apart the geopolitical conditions created by globalization. But we would have to be blind to think it all started on February 24. Actually, social civilization has been slowly eroded over the last forty years by a cult of economic profit, of frenzied intensification of exploitation, and of overall competition.

War and Rituals

While Hillman emphasizes the mythological backstage of the terrible love for war, Barbara Ehrenreich, in her book *Blood Rites*, emphasizes its ritual dimension. First she remarks that war is a ritual of access to the masculine gender: "War is, in fact, one of the most rigidly 'gendered' activities known

---

4   James Hillman (2004) *A Terrible Love of War*, Penguin.

to humankind."[5] But she adds that war is not the exclusive activity of males.

In fact, this ritual has not only a symbolic function, but an economic one too. War has played a role in the business of survival since hunters-gatherers were competing for the same territory. Nevertheless, it is a ritual that implies emotions like fear, aggressiveness, and hate — emotions that have nothing to do with the economic finality.

Plato, quoted by Ehrenreich, asserts that civilization was originally aimed at protecting the human species from aggressive animals. Technical ferocity spreads from animal ferocity:

> First, men lived apart from each other and no city existed. Because of this they were destroyed by animals that were always and everywhere stronger than they, and their industry that sufficed to feed them was yet inadequate to fight against the wild animals.[6]

The economic dimension (survival) and symbolic dimension (ritual) are mutually reinforcing in the genealogy of war. The economic function of war was not observed or analyzed by Marx, as Ehrenreich writes:

> Contrary to Marx, it is not only the "means of production" that shape human societies, but the means of destruction, and for much of human history the means of destruction have favored societies ruled by warriors themselves.[7]

---

5   Barbara Ehrenreich (2020) *Blood Rites: Origins and History of the Passions of War*, Grand Central Publishing, p. 152.

6   Quoted in *Ibid.*, p. 40.

7   *Ibid.*, p. 177.

I would argue that the Marx's theory is not totally oblivious to the productive role that war plays in the accumulation of capital, as the implications of the crisis of overproduction show. But this is not the point here.

Fundamentally, Ehrenreich's book is important because it aims to pinpoint the complementarity of the economic and psycho-symbolic sides of the rituals of war. The economic choice is between being predator or prey, and psycho-symbolic rituality helps to overcome the sense of helplessness that comes from being prey:

> Grief, depression, helplessness — these are the experiences of prey. The obvious way out, the way our species learned through a million years of conflict with larger and stronger animals, is to assume the stance of the predator: Turn grief to rage, go from listless mourning to the bustling preparations for offensive attack. This, more or less, is what Achilles does in the Iliad: He recovers from the paralysis of hurt feelings and grief through his spectacular revenge for Patroklus's death.[8]

Furthermore, Ehrenreich observes the link between the evolution of society and the evolution of weapons and war technology at large. Since the times of Cervantes, the democratization of modern societies has run parallel to the technological transformation of war:

> Where the elite warrior's goal was to close with an individual enemy and defeat him in single combat, now the bow or the gun propelled inanimate missiles at an enemy whose features

---

8   *Ibid.*, pp. 171–2

might never be visible. The killer and the killed could be many yards away from each.[9]

Then, in late modern times, this technology evolved to the point of allowing the de-personalization of war through the automation of killing:

> Missile-based warfare favored mass, sub-elite armies in another way, too: It made killing an impersonal business, requiring little motivation on the part of the individual gunner or bowman. The missile-bearing foot soldier did not meet his enemy with a shouted *défi*, or challenge, in which each announced his noble lineage; he did not have to meet him at all, since he barely had to see him to make him a target.[10]

Paul Virilio has focused on the technical development of the rituals of war, particularly linking military progress with the acceleration of the killing machine, the fast transportation of troops, air dominance, and hyper-speed missiles. In his book *Speed and Politics*, Paul Virilio speaks of the technical development of war, particularly linking military progress with the acceleration of the killing machine, the fast transportation of troops, air dominance, and hyper-speed missiles

A Terrible Love of War

Let's go back to Hillman, who states that "war is the playground of the incalculable."[11]

In *War and Peace*, Andrei Bolkonsky compares chess

---

9   *Ibid.*, p. 221.
10   *Ibid.*
11   James Hillman, *A Terrible Love of War*, p. 6.

and the game of war, coming to the conclusion that they are fundamentally different:

> "They do say war is a bit like playing chess."
> "Yes it is," said Prince Andrei, "but there's one little difference. In chess you can take as long as you want over each move. You're beyond the limits of time. Oh, there is this one other difference: a knight is always stronger than a pawn, and two pawns are always stronger than one, whereas in war a battalion can sometimes be stronger than a division, and sometimes weaker than a company. You can never be sure of the relative strength of different forces. Believe me," he went on, "if anything really depended on what gets done at headquarters, I'd be up there with them, doing things, but no, I have the honor of serving here in this regiment along with these gentlemen, and I'm convinced that tomorrow's outcome depends on us, not on them. Success never has depended, never will depend, on dispositions or armaments, not even numbers, and position least of all."
> "Well, what does it depend on?"
> "On the gut feeling inside me and him," he indicated Timokhin, "and every soldier."[12]

I don't think we have to choose between Marxism's explanation of war (the insistence on conflicting interests for fundamentally economic reasons), complemented by Reich's sex-economy (the repression of the sexual drive, the stiffening of character armor), and that proposed by Hillman, wherein war is not the effect of repression, but the natural expression of the collective

---

12 Leo Tolstoy (2005) *War and Peace*, trans. Anthony Briggs, Penguin Classics, p. 858.

unconscious which only education can remedy, always provisionally. I share both views. Instead, I am interested in the psychic dynamic that triggers war, as well as the socio-cultural dynamic that mobilizes natural aggressiveness and breaks the fragile constructions of language, compassion, and attraction for the other.

Hate is not the adversary of *Eros*, but the inevitable, irreversible outcome of its frustration. In liberal circles, there is talk of forbidding and punishing so-called hate speech. This is a meaningless project. Hate cannot be forbidden, and punishing hate means the persecution of sentiments, thoughts, and words. Hate can be healed and aggressiveness can be prevented once we are able to disentangle *Eros* (and *Ethos*) from external repression and intimate frustration. In order to do so, we need a better understanding of the context in which frustration is the norm.

From Repression to Hyper-Stimulation

As we have seen, in *The Mass Psychology of Fascism* Reich describes national or racist aggression as the effect of a stiffening of the character armor produced by sexual repression. Reich's intuition of a profound relationship between psycho-sexual alienation and aggression is to be welcomed; but today we exist in a psycho-political situation quite different from bourgeois society, the nuclear family, and the repression of non-monogamous sexuality that Reich describes. Instead, the prevailing injunction in the sphere of neoliberal semio-capitalism, conveyed by advertising, is: consumption with no limit. The promise of limitless enjoyment. Our experience has shown that this injunction has a pathogenic effect. The widespread ideology of boundlessness is pathogenic.

In order to understand our contemporary psycho-politics,

we first have to figure out what happened in the psychosphere of the first post-alphabetic generations, those who learned more words from machines than from their mothers. We must reframe our understanding of the unconscious and investigate the third unconscious,[13] which is no longer configured around neurosis, but on the psychotic dynamic unleashed by the neoliberal and digital acceleration.

Repression was the core of the Freudian scheme. Repression, neurosis, and the Reichian stiffening of the character armor. No more — now we face a profoundly different picture: neoliberal capitalism has produced an injunction to consume every available good, has reduced the body to a commodity between commodities, and has promoted unlimited enjoyment as the norm, while at the same time making enjoyment increasingly unattainable. This has produced a sort of emotional overload with paradoxical effects of anxiety and psychosis.

Cellular ubiquity, the availability of devices that make permanent connection possible, is now likely causing the destructuration of the very cognitive capacity of the iPhone generation. Child psychiatrists have been describing attention disorders since the 1990s, but as far as I know, one essential point has rarely been grasped: the acceleration, intensification, and ubiquity of neuro-informative stimulus is provoking an inability to disconnect the mental flow from external stimulus, and as an autonomous stream of consciousness.

Perpetual connection, constant interaction with the screen, daily participation in games that do not involve the presence of other players — these widespread behaviors are mutating the nature of human communication, but also, at a deeper level, the very fabric of cognitive activity.

---

13 Franco Berardi (2022) *The Third Unconscious: The Psychosphere in the Viral Age*, Verso.

Neuropsychiatrists have tried to explain attention deficit disorders in organic terms:

> Children with the truly inattentive type of ADHD, rather than being distractible, may instead be easily bored, their problem being more in motivation (underarousal) than in inhibitory control. Much converging evidence points to a primary disturbance in the striatum (a frontal-striatal loop) in the combined type of ADHD. It is proposed here that the primary disturbance in truly inattentive-type ADHD (ADD) is in the cortex (a frontal-parietal loop).[14]

In 1995, Orlando Villegas described this emerging disease in his essay "Understanding Attention Deficit Disorders":

> These children usually act before thinking. It is usually not an intentionally disruptive behavior [...] they have a difficult time inhibiting behavior. This impulse control deficiency seems to have a biological origin. This means that they react impulsively without stopping to think about the consequences of the behavior, beginning new activities before they have completed the previous one.[15]

When it comes to pointing out the causes of this disorder, or at least the context in which this disorder has become more prevalent, Villegas seems disoriented:

---

14 "Attention-deficit disorder (attention-deficit/hyperactivity disorder without hyperactivity): A neurobiologically and behaviorally distinct disorder from attention-deficit/hyperactivity disorder (with hyperactivity)," *Development and Psychopathology*, 2005; 17(3): 807–25, doi:10.1017/S0954579405050388.

15 Orlando Villegas, "Understanding Attention Deficit Disorders," *Oakland County Schools*, Pontiac, Mich. Div. of Special Education, March 1995.

> These children have a hard time when they are requested to pay attention. They have no problems paying attention to something that is funny, or just interesting. This is why they can watch TV or play video games for hours without interruption. This attention problem is mostly evidenced in the classroom setting. ADHD children are unable to sustain attention on what the teacher is showing, writing on the board or on their seatwork.[16]

Villegas seems totally unaware of the link and the difference between two different media: the teacher's words in the classroom have a neuro-stimulative power that is different from the neuro-stimulative power of electronic immersion. The rhythm of stimulation is different, the bodily implication is different. So persuading a student to pay attention to the teacher may be as difficult as persuading a heroin addict to replace their white powder with orange juice. It does not work.

As Marshall McLuhan described it in 1964 in *Understanding Media*: When social communication shifts from the sequentiality of the written word to the simultaneity of the electronic flow, the mind tunes in to a different rhythm of processing.[17]

Following Villegas's pioneering text, some authors have grasped the link between the technosphere of communication and attention disorders. Jean Twenge, in her book *iGen*, provides a mass of data on the relationship between cellular connection time and psychic fragility, particularly regarding disturbances in attention to non-electronic flows.[18] In *The*

---

16 *Ibid.*

17 Marshall McLuhan (1964) *Understanding Media: The Extensions of Man*, McGraw-Hill

18 Jean Twenge, *iGen.*

Shallows, Nicholas Carr outlines this process of mutation using the tools of psychology and sociology, as well as his personal experience:

> The very way my brain worked seemed to be changing. It was then that I began worrying about my inability to pay attention to one thing for more than a couple of minutes. At first I'd figured that the problem was a symptom of middle-age mind rot. But my brain, I realized, wasn't just drifting. It was hungry. It was demanding to be fed the way the Net fed it — and the more it was fed, the hungrier it became. Even when I was away from my computer, I yearned to check e-mail, click links, do some Googling. [19]

However, Carr was an adult when he began to navigate the Internet — his neuro-cognitive system was already formed. Instead, we are thinking about a generation who have been *formed* in an immersive electronic environment, who learn more words from machines than from their mothers or brothers, and who spend most of their time in close interaction with digital neural stimuli. What are (and what will be) the effects of this cognitive (and perhaps neurological) mutation, which we cannot interrupt or influence?

A child who has access to a cell phone with video games from its earliest years, who spends several hours every day in front of the screen, cannot be suddenly deprived of it. I have personally witnessed children in hysterics, screaming, experiencing inconsolable despair when their parents have for some reason stolen the device from them and stopped its neuro-stimulating flow. They weren't having a tantrum; they

---

19 Nicholas Carr (2010) *The Shallows: What the Internet Is Doing to Our Brains*, Norton, p. 25.

were reacting with the desperation of a drug addict barred from accessing the substance they depend on. What portion of the child population is already neuro-dependent? Are we already beyond the point of no return in this process of de-activating emphatic intelligence?

The Psychological Roots of the Contemporary Ethical Catastrophe

Consumerism, an injunction to the enjoinment and unattainability of pleasure, a mutation of the techno-communication context: these factors have changed the horizon in which psycho-sexual energies are invested, the psycho-political landscape of our time.

The pandemic also deployed a psycho-mutagenic process: a phobic awareness of the other's body that favors, indeed even urges, social distancing. The technologies that make such a distancing possible have spread over the lived time of the generation that defines itself as the last.

The digital network intensifies the stimulus and simultaneously reduces the time of erotic proximity. The faculty of language is transformed by technology as the mother's body and voice are replaced by the digital machine in the access to language. By the word "mother," I mean the body that speaks, the body that introduces the singularity of language, not the biological mother who takes care of the child born from her womb. That body is the body which emits signification; it is the warmth and singular vibration of the voice.

I've established a lasting relationship between ethics and sympathy, and now I assert that sympathy is a manifestation of sensibility, that is, of pre-verbal receptivity to the presence of the other (of the erotic body, of the aesthetic form).

Consequently, I recognize that the ethical values of modern civilization, founded on Enlightened universalism, are exposed for what they truly are: ineffective norms that can only become actionable thanks to the enforcement of repressive organs like the state, the family, and most of all the bank.

A psycho-cognitive mutation is taking place on the anthropological horizon of the new generations that are today growing up in a connective, digital sphere. This mutation is transforming the very conditions of individuation, of the singularization of the experience, and therefore the perception, of the other's body.

I propose to conceptualize what David Hume calls sympathy as a synthesis of sensibility and sensitivity. By sensibility, I mean the faculty of grasping the meaning of what cannot be expressed in words, and by sensitivity, the faculty of feeling the skin of the other as a pleasure or as an annoyance, pain, or indifferent fact. This living synthesis of sensibility and sensitivity enables the perception of the other as a sensible continuity of the self, extended to the body of the planet, to the body of the human kind, to the body of the city, of the village, of the square, of the community.

In the context of patriarchal culture and the capitalist economy, *Eros* has been opposed to ethics and self-pleasure, and therefore reduced to a mere accumulation of property, power, capital. For this reason, its ethical dimension has historically been weakened and constrained in the sphere of duty, of the law, of the abstract norm.

However, if in the sphere of capitalism and patriarchal culture the separation of ethics from *Eros* was achieved through imposition and the repression of the transgressive, today, following the psycho-anthropological mutation induced by digital technology, that separation is no longer enforced by repressive threats. It has instead invaded the sphere of desire and shaped its expectations. Consequently, inter-personal relations are reduced to social contracts in which one is indebted to the other — one is exploited and the other accumulates profit. In this condition, self-love is made incompatible with love of the other.

From a materialist point of view, ethics is not based on any normative value, but on the perception of the body of others as a sensitive continuation of one's own. Therefore, the possibility of an ethical life is wrecked when competition takes the place of empathy in the social sphere.

What we are experiencing today — in a time when war (which had never disappeared from the planet) has returned to center stage, sweeping Europe, jeopardizing the global economy, and contributing to the final devastation of the planetary environment — is an ethical catastrophe.

The Russian aggression against the population of Ukrainian towns and villages, and equally the decision of the Atlantic powers to arm the Ukrainian Army to prolong the massacre, is evidence of this long-prepared ethical catastrophe. This ethical catastrophe is also a consequence of a psychic paralysis caused by a sort of generalized autistic syndrome: the inability to feel pleasure at the pleasure of the other, and to feel pain at the pain of the other. The other is reduced to an economic competitor, an enrichment tool to be exploited, and in the end an enemy to be annihilated.

Can we talk about a normalization of the autistic syndrome? Or perhaps we must recognize that so-called autism is not a pathology of the mind, but rather a difficult attempt by the mind to achieve a non-empathic balance in an environment that is becoming more and more psychically and aesthetically intolerable. The neuro-psychiatrist Stefano Mistura describes clinical autism with words that seem to perfectly capture our contemporary psycho-political framework: "Autistic people [...] are not capable of empathy and do not have a theory of the mind of others."[20]

We must acknowledge that the term "autism," now identified with a mental disorder, no longer captures the substance of the problem, and indeed hides the fact that behavior we might label autistic in the sense intended above, is now often regarded as normal.

It's important to remark that autism has been diagnosed more and more often since the 1990s, when free-market economic competition and digital distancing became the social norm. In 1976, there were around four or five cases of autism out of every ten thousand children under the age of 15.[21] In 2014, the Centers for Disease Control of the United States attested that the syndrome occurs in 1 in 68 girls, and 1 in 40 boys.[22]

Of course, this increase in numbers is partly due to a refinement of diagnostic skills, but based on the experience of educators and doctors, we can also attest that the explosion of this pathology referred to as autistic syndrome is real. How can we explain this explosion, if not by starting from the changed nature of inter-personal relationships in a context profoundly

---

20 Stefano Mistura (2006) *Autismo. L'umanità nascosta*, Einaudi.

21 L. Wing, S.R. Yeates, L.M. Brierley, and J .Gould, "The Prevalence of Early Childhood Autism: Comparison of Administrative and Epidemiological Studies," *Psychol Med*, 1976 Feb; 6(1): 89–100. doi: 10.1017/s0033291700007522.

22 Centers for Disease Control, *Community Report on Autism*, 2014. Available online at: https://www.cdc.gov/ncbddd/autism/states/comm_report_autism_2014.pdf

modified by technologies of distancing and an economy increasingly based on competition between physically isolated and functionally connected individuals?

Psychologists speak of "theory of the other's mind," and assert that the autistic person is devoid of this theory, or at least scarcely provided with it. However, it must be said that this "theory of the other's mind," this empathic perception of the other's presence as emotionally and cognitively motivated, is *not a natural given*, but the outcome of a long-lasting exchange in which language and affectivity are not separated but interwoven and confirm each other. When the cognitive formation and the affective formation are disjoined, when we grow up in a network of techno-cognitive automatisms, we are no longer led to assume the existence of the mind of the other, or of the emotionality of the other. What is required is only the interpretation of signs that come from the other organism. There is no need to acknowledge the emotional background and the affective intentionality of those signs.

The code that enables the interpretation of signs is a digital one that overlooks non-verbal interaction. Consequently, in connective conditions we are led to interact without perceiving or postulating the existence of the other as a conscious and sensible organism.

More and more we communicate with non-existing interlocutors; more and more a machine (a troll, an automaton) hides behind meaningful interactions. But regardless of the bodily and emotional existence of the interlocutor, our brain is affected by the act of processing the signs, and our mind is semantically interpreting these stimuli. This transformation of communication into automatic interaction cannot happen without an ethical disturbance. In an ethical relation, in fact, the wellbeing of the enunciator cannot be separated from the wellbeing of the receiver who is called to interpret, and vice versa. This syntony cannot be the effect of a legal norm, of an injunction of an authority, or of a moralistic lecture. In order to elaborate strategies for treating or avoiding the current ethical catastrophe, we must first understand the psycho-cultural context within which this catastrophe is maturing: the mediasphere has taken full command of the psychosphere, and this erodes our capacity for affective and bodily interaction.

And we have also to go back to the epistemic context: modernity has progressively developed an obsessive way of projecting into the future, that is, of imagining, because expansion has become the only imaginable horizon and has turned into a general epistemic rule, the guiding principle of every technology and every expectation.

The psycho-cultural introjection of the expansion principle by the Western mind has produced a fixation on increasing productivity, acceleration, and expansion of the production base as the only acceptable paths forward. It has also removed death from the scene of the social imagination. In fact, in the Western mind, accumulation works as a guarantee of eternity, of the priority of the abstract disembodied value over the perishable concrete.

This psycho-cultural fixation is at the root of our current inability to accept and process the exhaustion of the physical and nervous energies that made capitalist growth and expansion possible.

Trans-Humanism and
Geronto-Fascism

I have lost my sight, smell, hearing, taste and touch:
How should I use them for your closer contact?
These with a thousand small deliberations
Protract the profit of their chilled delirium,
Excite the membrane, when the sense has cooled.

T.S. Eliot, "Gerontion"

The cultural environment in which fascism emerged in the first decades of the twentieth century was futurist and euphoric: Mussolini's regime represented the reaction of a young population, of veterans coming back from World War I, suffering for the humiliation inflicted by the victors of the war, who at Versailles had scornfully ignored the demands of the young Italian nation. Fascism emerged as revenge, turning an impending depression into a violent euphoria, projecting Italy towards colonial adventures that were no less bankrupt than bloody, until it plunged the country into World War II. As for the Germans, they lived through the 1930s in a state of failure and economic (and above all moral) misery, and recovered from that condition when Hitler launched an aggressive campaign aiming to war and to extermination. Humiliation, revenge, youth, and aggressive energy: these are the pre-requisites of fascism.

Some of these pre-requisites are visible in our present scenario, one hundred years after the victory of Mussolini in Italy. However, the European people of the twenty-first century are no longer young. On the contrary, Alzheimer's disease is spreading in its ageing population: the bellicose euphorias that run through a (minority) part of the European population should be read as a sign of senile dementia: sudden outbursts of fury and enthusiasm followed by real amnesia. Think of the excitement of the Euro-American press and intellectual establishment when they went to the war in Afghanistan in 2001: the destiny of civilization and democracy depended on that war. Then the war got bogged down for twenty years, and eventually the Americans and their allies had to sadly leave, while panic and chaos erupted in Kabul. But who remembers that story?

What we witness today is the *futurism of the old*, a movement without energy and without memory, a false movement that causes reckless euphoria and sets in motion destructive energies that the geronto-futurist mind cannot control, in the end provoking catastrophic effects and worsening the depression it was intended to cure.

Annihilate

Anéantir, the Michel Houellebecq novel published in 2022, is not his best, but it does succeed in sketching a simultaneously hopeless and irate representation of the decline of the white race and of its supremacy.

In deep France, a family gathers around their eighty-year-old father, who has suffered a stroke. The patriarch, who had worked for the secret service, has now fallen into an interminable coma. Meanwhile, his son Paul, who also works for the secret service as well as for the Ministry of Finance, discovers he has terminal cancer. The other son, Aurélien, Paul's brother, kills himself, being incapable of continuing a life in which he has always been considered a loser. The daughter, Cécile, is a Catholic fundamentalist married to a fascist notary who has lost his job but found another in the right-wing circle of the Lepenists, still on the rise.

The central theme of the novel is terminal illness — in other words it is about the agony of Western civilization. Not a pretty sight, because the white mind does not resign itself to the inescapable. Tragic is the reaction of the agonizing old white men.

The novel's story takes place in contemporary France — a place that has been culturally devasted over the last forty years of neoliberal aggression. It is a ghost of a country in which political struggle now takes place in the corrupt squares of ultra-nationalism, racism, islamophobia, and economic fundamentalism. But this is not only true of France; it is the condition of the post-global world, one now threatened by the senile delirium of the dominant culture as it falls — that of the white, Christian, imperialist empire.

In the age of mutually assured destruction, war cannot be explained in strategic terms. We don't need to think geopolitically in order to understand war. We need to think in psycho-pathological terms: we need a geopolitics of psychotic outbursts.

At stake is the political, economic, demographic, and finally psychic defeat of white, Western, (post-)colonial civilization, which cannot accept the prospect of exhaustion, and which prefers destruction or suicide to the slow extinction of white dominance.

I define the West as a sphere of racist dominance obsessed with the future. Time stretches out in an expansive pulse:

economic growth, accumulation, capitalism. It is exactly this obsession with the future that feeds the machine of dominance: a concrete present (of pleasure, of muscular relaxation) is invested into and exchanged for abstract future value. Perhaps we could reformulate the classical Marxist analysis of value to say that exchange value is precisely this accumulation of the present (the concrete) in abstract forms (like money) that can be exchanged for something else tomorrow.

The fixation and fetishization of the future are by no means a natural cognitive modality of the human — most human cultures have been organized around a cyclical understanding of time, or on the insuperable dilation of the present. Futurism is a transition to complete self-consciousness (also in aesthetic terms) of cultures of expansion. But there are many futurisms.

The obsession with the future has different implications in the theological-utopian sphere that is central to Russian culture and the techno-economic sphere in Euro-American culture. Federov's cosmism and Mayakovski's futurism have an eschatological breath lacked by the technocratic fanaticism of Marinetti and Musk. Maybe that's why it's Russia's destiny to end history—and here we are.

Nazism Everywhere

Past the pandemic threshold, the new horizon is a global fragmentary war that pits one Nazism against another. In his writings from the 1960s, Günther Anders predicted that the nihilistic charge of Nazism would not die with the defeat of Hitler. He presaged that it would return to the world stage due to the magnification of technical power provoking the humiliation of the human will made impotent.

Today, Nazism is reemerging as a psycho-political form of the demented body of the white race furiously reacting to its own unstoppable decline. Viral chaos has created the conditions for the formation of a global, biopolitical infrastructure, but it has also accentuated the widely experienced perception of matter's ungovernability.

The West has forsaken death because it is not compatible with its obsession with the future. It has rejected senility because it is not compatible with expansion and growth. But now, the (demographic, cultural, and economic) ageing of the dominant cultures of the Global North is a specter that white culture cannot even think of, let alone accept.

This is where the white brain (both Biden's and Putin's) enters a furious crisis of senile dementia. Donald Trump utters a truth that no one can stand to bear: Putin is our best friend. Trump means that he's a racist murderer, but we are no less so. On the other hand, Biden represents the impotent anger that old people express and feel when they notice the decline of their strength, psychic energy, and cognitive efficiency. Now that exhaustion is in its advanced stage, extinction is the only reassuring prospect. Can humanity save itself from the murderous violence of the demented and agonized Western, Russian, and European brains?

In the suicidal war that one West is waging against the Other West, the first victims are those who have suffered from the deliriums of both spheres of influence and power — those who want no war but are made miserable by its effects.

The final war against humanity has begun. The only thing we can do is desert, abandon, collectively transform fear into thought, resign ourselves to the inevitable, and create a line of escape.

Trans-humanism as Ideology and Technique

If Italian futurism was the exaltation of technical speed and male power, Russian futurism was the aspiration to a cosmic projection of energy that merged with the Soviet Revolution viewed as a utopia. The common mission of the two different futurisms was the conquest of the future, boundless expansion in the fields of technology and economy, and the colonization of the planet.

What has changed since the first futurist era is easy to say: expansion is no longer in the range of technical and economic possibility. Growth has reached its limit because the planet's physical resources are running out and because humans have been subjected to intolerable stress from the competitive acceleration of neoliberalism.

The contemporary version of futurism takes the name "trans-humanism" and the form of a hysterical delusion: the brain and the body are rotting, morally and physically, but in the process they express a sort of Alzheimer's futurism. According to some trans-humanist theorists, especially in North America, trans-humanism aims to emancipate the body, or at least the brain, from its biological limits, namely from the deterioration provoked by the passing of time. This project can be realized by transferring the organism's functions into technological devices.

This is the aim of one of the most important theorists of high-tech trans-humanism, Max More, who in his "Letter to Mother Nature (Amendments to Human Constitution)," with a style reminiscent of Marinetti's grandiloquence and aggressiveness, writes, addressing nature:

> We will no longer tolerate the tyranny of ageing and death. Through genetic alterations, cellular manipulations, synthetic

organs, and any necessary means, we will endow ourselves with enduring vitality and remove our expiration date. We will each decide for ourselves how long we shall live.[1]

There is something repugnant in the intrinsic racial elitism of this project, a project which is luckily not so realistic. Those who might allow themselves to receive enhanced brains would be the members of the elite, who are already profiting from costly medical technologies to which the majority of people have no access. Aside from this non-irrelevant detail, the philosophy of Max More is based on a flawed understanding of the relationship between conscious organisms and temporality. What would happen in the life of this trans-human individual whose a-temporality More is celebrating in his manifesto? What ocean of eternal sadness would trans-human people navigate? When I read More's icy neo-futurist delirium, I cannot refrain from considering the spread of Alzheimer's in the senescent population of the Northern Hemisphere.

Alzheimer's syndrome is the effect of the degradation of brain tissues. Perhaps a remedy will be found for this degradation and the pathology it causes, but Alzheimer's is also a metaphor for the relationship between the mind, organically located in the temporality of a body, and the incessant chaotic proliferation of reality.

The mind constructs its orders, its expectations, its plans, and calls it the cosmos. But the cosmos is constantly attacked by chaos, and the mind has to protect itself from it, but

---

1 Max More (2009) "A Letter to Mother Nature: Amendments to the Human Constitution," *Max More's Strategic Philosophy*. Available online at: https://strategicphilosophy.blogspot.com/2009/05/its-about-ten-years-since-i-wrote.html

at the same time it has to tune into chaos, to recompose it chaosmotically.

The origin and cause of this continuous exchange, recombination, and dissipation is time, which the trans-humanist neuroengineers are not able to abolish. This is why the trans-humanist ideology is devoid of subtlety, devoid of depth, and devoid of irony. It is an ideology produced by the techno-economic elite of a country that is terrified by the prospect of death and which therefore is destined from the outset to spread death, violence, slavery, racial and social oppression, and sexual and psychological brutality.

The place where this ideology of techno-eternity has emerged is a country that has made genocide and slavery the condition of its prosperity, and which is now planning immortality for itself and for its children. Meanwhile in that same country, from the mass shooting at Columbine High School in 1999 onwards, a growing and unstoppable wave of mass shootings and suicides has been spreading.

Psychotic slaughter and techno-immortality are two sides of the same worldview. The first arouses horror, but also sadness and a great deal of compassion. The second, as far as I'm concerned, only arouses horror and contempt.

A Short History of Happiness

There are no precise gauges of happiness and unhappiness. Actually, we don't even know what we mean by these words. However, even though we don't know exactly what we are talking about, many signs show that the rate of happiness has never been so low, particularly among women. According to the PEW Research Center in 2023, female students continue to be at a higher risk for suicidal thoughts and behaviors than their male counterparts. Three in ten females surveyed (30 percent) said that they had seriously considered attempting suicide in the past year, and nearly a quarter (24 percent) had made a suicide plan. This represents a 60 percent increase in both measures over the past decade. During the same period, suicide attempts by female students increased by 30 percent.[1] These trends are exposing an epidemic of mental disease that overshadows the psycho-scape of the first generation that has learned more words from machines than from their mothers.

The Factory of Unhappiness

The moderns searched for happiness in the order of history, conceiving of it as the fulfillment of a project or the overcoming of present contradictions.

In the last decades of the twentieth century, as the political

---

1   Farzana Akkas, "Youth Suicide Risk Increased Over Past Decade," *PEW Research Center*, 3 March 2023. Available online at: https://www.pewtrusts.org/en/research-and-analysis/articles/2023/03/03/youth-suicide-risk-increased-over-past-decade

promise was dissolving, the electronic glare announced the new horizon of happiness: boundless connection, virtual immersion, competition, and freedom of enterprise. The marriage of economy and digital technology paved the way to unbounded expansion of consumption and communication. This was the postmodern way to happiness. The ideology of liberation was translated into deregulation — rules were broken such that only one rule remained: the rule of competition, which made precarious every human relation and every expectation of the future.

As a mirror of impoverished life, the screen multiplied ubiquitously to enable unrelenting communication, and in the mirror everyone drew their imaginary self-portrait, free from the myths of community and belonging.

This is the age of *advertising*.

The screen obliged everybody to pay ceaseless attention and to devote all energies to the pursuit of a dream that consumes the consumer. In the end, we realized that happiness is only possible on screen.

This is the age of *reality*.

Finally, a generation grew up directly onscreen, a generation that has learned the meaning of signs from the screen such that the meaning of bodily contact remains undecipherable.

This is the age of the *social network*.

Simulated sociality.

Communist Unhappiness

The revolutionary movements of the past century left the imaginary territory of happiness in the hands of capitalism. This, possibly, is the main reason for their defeat. Communist revolution started off on the wrong foot, and mostly in the wrong place.

The religious culture of the Russian Orthodox Church views the body as a crime that finds in itself its own punishment. The possession of a body is the source of perpetual suffering, and pain is the deserved punishment for the guilt of existing, of having been born into this horrible place that is the Earth, particularly in the most horrible place of all, Russia. The Russian rhetoric of beauty must be read in reverse, as a manifestation of the masochistic orthodox taste for self-inflicted suffering.

Russian writers sing the infinite agony of living beings, and they call this infinite pain joy. Dostoevsky writes: "The most basic, most rudimentary spiritual need of the Russian people is the need for suffering, ever-present and unquenchable, everywhere and in everything."[2]

Leninism is also by no means immune from the cult of pain and the fanaticism of purity. On the contrary, it is its apotheosis. Central to the Leninist conception is the belief that the party must constantly purge itself of any relationship with the impure substance of real life, because the party is the embodiment of pure idea. The Soviet Revolution caused a perennial laceration in the body of society, and forced revolutionary workers around the world to defend a totalitarian state and to be part of a war whose principle was the purity of the revolutionary idea. That war lasted until 1989, but defeat was inevitable from the start. It may be that Leninist-Bolshevism has ruined Russia, which has never been such a cheerful place anyway. What is certain is that Russia has ruined communism as a possible alternative to capitalism.

---

2 Fyodor Dostoevsky (2009) *A Writer's Diary*, Northwestern University Press.

Capitalism will certainly be horrible, workers around the world told themselves, but if the alternative is Lenin's hell, then there is no alternative.

The movements of the 1960s and '70s desperately tried to free themselves from the legacy of Leninist communism, but ended up getting sucked into the abyss. "Happiness is subversive when it becomes collective," said the *Indiani Metropolitani* and the MaoDadaist rebels of the 1977 Movement, taking up the thread of hippy culture that in the 1960s had already scandalously shouted that the orgasm is more important than the war in Vietnam. There was no cynicism in that claim — it voiced the awareness that war is a manifestation of a collective anorgasmia, and that if you want to eradicate war, you need to deal with happiness, with the pleasure of the encounter between bodies.

The Era of Sad Passions

Les passions tristes: souffrance psychique et crise sociale (*Sad Passions: Psychological Suffering and Social Crisis*) is the title of a book in which Miguel Benasayag and Gérard Schmidt, drawing on their twenty years' experience of psychoanalytic practice in the Parisian suburbs, speak of the prevailing sentiment in the era of precarity. According to them, the era of sad passions coincides with the era in which the future is no longer perceived as a promise, but as a threat. It is the era of precarity, which extends from the sphere of employment relationships to the entire spectrum of collective psychology, and to the imaginary field of expectations for the future.

To delimit the time of sad contemporaneity, I would start from the year 1977. As the smoothness of the immaterial moved to the center of sensible experience and communication, the material world and physical experience began to be perceived as "*kipple*," a word invented by Philip K. Dick to indicate the dusty residues of decaying matter. As communication began to shift into the smooth sphere of the digital, physicality became residue and dust. Nineteen seventy-seven was the year in which this separation of the smooth and the dusty made its appearance, in music and in visual culture, with punk and new wave experimentalism.

Nineteen seventy-seven was a two-sided year. It was the year of the last proletarian uprisings of the century, but also the year in which Steve Wozniak and Steve Jobs registered the Apple brand. It was also the year that Alain Minc and Simon Nora wrote *L'informatisation de la société*, a report on the computerization of society, which predicted the imminent dissolution of the nation state as an effect of emerging telematics. And at the end of the year, Charlie Chaplin died — as the man with the bowler hat and walking stick went away, the last traces of kindness disappeared with him. The insurrection that broke out in Italy during that year spoke the language of desire and was aimed at happiness. Precisely because the desiring movement had made happiness its content, the movement's end coincided with the painful emergence of an oppressive unhappiness.

Saturday Night Fever, also released that year, marked a turning point in the history of youth behavior and rock culture, and was the signal of a defeat: we can no longer aspire to a happy dimension for everyday life, we must accept the idea that the week is made up of sad days, and only on Saturday evening can we unleash our energy within spaces destined for temporary joy, limited in time and space. Disco music competed with punk for the musical listening space of that transition.

It was also the year that a group of German filmmakers, under the collective signature of Filmverlag der Autoren, produced *Deutschland im Herbst* (*Germany in Autumn*), which chronicled the effects of terrorism on society and social movements, the darkening cultural climate of the mid-to-late 1970s, and the exhaustion of an existential dimension in which the happy sharing of living spaces was possible. Rainer Werner Fassbinder, a member of Filmverlag der Autoren, continued this exploration of terrorism in his 1979 film *Die Dritte Generation* (*The Third Generation*), which opens with the following description: "A comedy in 6 parts, full of tension, excitement and logic, cruelty and madness. Similar to the fairytales we tell our children to help them endure their lives until death."

The political defeat of the liberatory movements of the twentieth century is only the surface of an anthropological mutation that has traversed all forms of life. Their vision was then occupied by the screen, the unconscious colonized by the mediascape, and desire perverted by competition.

The Italian 1977 Movement had shouted it: happiness is subversive when it becomes collective. But unfortunately, in the following years, we learned about the reverse of that promise. When energy and solidarity ebb, happiness becomes impossible as a collective horizon. From that moment, the collapse of the Western mind followed an episodic, underground trajectory; then, at the threshold of the millennium, it took on a precipitous rhythm: the collapse of the Twin Towers in a cloud of dust was certainly a spectacular inauguration of these new times. The Columbine High School massacre that took place only two years earlier contained an even more disturbing message.

In the first decade of the new century in Japan, a true laboratory of contemporary alienation, a reclusive behavior spread. It was called "*hikikomori*" — voluntary self-confinement in one's bedroom. The hikikomori suspends all relations with his peers and limits himself to virtual relationships. For the Japanese state, this was a social problem to be kept under control: in 2008, the official estimates recorded about seven hundred thousand people definable as hikikomori; in the following years, the official figure reached one and a half million.[3] Officially, this behavior is treated as a pathology, but the choice to lock oneself in one's room and interrupt all social relationships is perfectly understandable in a competitive society where social relationships are a source of constant stress and discomfort.

Virtual Happiness and Real Solitude

The creation of the digital network was preceded by an advertising campaign that identified energy with economic competition, and competition with speed in network connection. Digitization has produced a double effect: it has turned work into a game and simultaneously subjected the game to the economy. Work is fragmented and disseminated in the interstices of daily life so as to enable ubiquitous precariousness.

Dave Eggars' 2013 novel *The Circle* takes place inside an office where twelve thousand cognitive workers produce the services provided by the world's largest company, a sort of conglomerate that brings together Facebook, Twitter, Google, PayPal, YouTube, and more. Eggars captures essential aspects of a world dominated by the obsession with transparency and the obligation to socialize. In this world, there is an outside and

---

3   "1.5 million people in Japan living as social recluses, many as a result of the pandemic," *Japan Times*, 1 April 2023. Available online at: https://www.japantimes.co.jp/news/2023/04/01/national/hikikomori-numbers-pandemic/

there is an inside. "Outside the walls of the Circle, everything is noise and conflict, failure and filth. But here everything is perfect."[4]

The cloying promise of perfection is fulfilled in the sphere of digital technology: those who make themselves perfectly transparent thanks to hundreds of millions of cameras distributed everywhere will become part of the perfect dream. "We will become able to see everything, to know everything, everything that happens will be known," says the protagonist, Mae, who is hired by to perform executive functions and quickly climbs to the top of the company to become the image that it presents to the world. *The Circle* is a fable about communication as a job that saturates every moment, forcing the individual into constant extroversion. The artificial needs that permanent connection arouses can only be satisfied by that permanent connection, in an endless spiral.

The Name of the Father and the Body of the Mother

Modernity has linked the singular experience of happiness with collective historical destiny, but history is not the place to seek happiness, as Freud argues in *Civilization and its Discontents*. Sublimation is a condition of access to the civilizing process, and the pleasure principle, which guides the conscious and unconscious choices of human beings, is in conflict with the whole world — "All the regulations of the universe run counter to it. One feels inclined to say that the intention that man should be 'happy' is not included in the plan of 'Creation.'"[5] The task of psychoanalysis is not

---

4   Dave Eggars (2013) *The Circle*, Knopf, p. 21.

5   Sigmund Freud, *Civilization and its Discontents*, in *The Standard Edition of the Complete Psychological Works of Sigmund Freud, Volume XXI (1927–1931): The Future of an Illusion, Civilization and its Discontents, and*

so much to get rid of discomfort as to put us in a position to consciously accept unhappiness, because analysis ends only when we realize the interminability of the analytic dialogue.

But in the climate of existential revolution that accompanied the explosion of 1968, psychoanalysis tried to get rid of the limits set by Freud. Following the path opened by Wilhelm Reich, many psychoanalysts sought a convergence between social liberation and the happy production of the unconscious. In *Anti-Oedipus*, Deleuze and Guattari said that the unconscious should not be seen as the theatre in which the drama of Oedipus and guilt takes place, but as a laboratory in which new imaginations, new existential possibilities are invented.

"Get rid of Oedipus and the paternal norm, and you will finally be free and happy": this is the message that many (including myself) took from that book in the 1970s. But it was too simple a reading, even if perhaps authorized by the text. We could not imagine that capital's offensive against social life would be based precisely on deregulation: the very liberation we had dreamed of paved the way to the hell of capitalist absolutism.

Rereading the writings of Deleuze and Guattari today, we understand that their conceptual device is not only the program of a happy liberation, but also the prefigurative cartography of neoliberal deterritorialization: the rhizome and the schizoid explosion of desire are the infernal modalities of the semi-productive flow and of precarious work.

After the great storm of 1968, emancipation resulted in the subjugation of female work: the feminization of work and precaritization are two parallel processes. The submission

---

Other Works, p. 433.

of female time acted as a factor of psychological change: the detachment of the child from the mother's body and the replacement of the mother's voice with the digital machine in the language-learning process make the relationship between bodies fragile and therefore precarious. Children grow up alone in an environment saturated with digital stimuli; they do not know the physical existence of their peers, and learn their words from a machine, as if words were operational functions of a purely linguistic system, and not affective matter.

The psycho-genesis of meaning is at stake here. Throughout human history, the meaning of words has been based on the affective authentication of the mother's body, of the voice that singularizes language. We are witnessing today the functional reduction of language, a rescission of the relation between meaning and vocal singularity. This is the core of precaritization: the relation between words and things is no longer based on affective confidence, on bodily sharing, but is reduced to an operational function. This is why people are unable to be friends.

So What?

Now the time has come to answer the question that I have evaded so far: What is happiness? How do we identify it, and how can we know when are experiencing it? Have we ever experienced it at all? How can we talk about it?

As far as I know, human beings experience happiness as a moment of conscious suspension of the abyss, as the creation of provisional bridges over it. I'm talking about the abyss of meaninglessness, which is also the abyss of failing. The absence of a foundation places us in front of the consciousness of death, of the decomposition of the self.

This is the abyss, but humans know how to traverse it

happily, holding hands as if they were walking over a bridge. The bridge over the abyss of meaninglessness is the dialogue that establishes the sharing of a feeling, a vision. Sensuous, sensible sharing liberates you from the fear of not being, and makes it possible to be in tune with the singular rhythm (the refrain of non-attachment). Free yourself from the will to live, and therefore live at last. This sensuous and sensible sharing takes the forms of falling in love, tenderness, creation, travel, hallucination, insurrection: movement. Each of these experiences is manifested above all as an experience of meaning.

Sense, which is both direction and meaning, is not given in nature, but only in consciousness, and consciousness experiences meaning as a sudden suspension of the original and founding dispersion. Sense is a sort of negentropy, suspension, or subversion of the heaviness of the continuous loss of order that living implies.

The stiffening of character armor, attachment to the self, is hindering the experience of sense that we sometimes call happiness. When the borders of identity weaken or possibly collapse, one can perceive the syntony of the singular drift and the cosmic game.

Sartre speaks of the "group-in-fusion" (*groupe en fusion*), referring to the harmonious relation with others in sharing solidarity. Guattari speaks of collective *d'enunciation*, referring to the harmony of singular *ritournelles* that happen to be tuned to the same frequency. By the word "movement," I refer to the utmost extension of this condition of happiness, whereby identity fades and almost vanishes, and meaning can flow, because we are no longer frightened by our own death.

The Missed Appointment

Modern history, as the history of the relationship between labor and capital, was at a certain point faced with the most fundamental alternative: I will call this the alternative between the idle and the industrious. The idle prefer to minimize their needs, and so, while having very little, they live in luxury. The industrious need to continually do something to escape the sense of guilt generated by the painful consciousness that time passes (as if it were someone's fault). The industrious are anxious persons who need to work because work, like any obsessive ritual, allows them to hold the world together, which otherwise dissolves into a disordered dust, while the idle have no anxieties, because they are not worried about dust. The industrious, the anxious, adore business because it allows them to forget their fear of the passing of time, and their fear (horror of emptiness) that this time is unemployed. They are willing to do anything to kill time: they therefore become CEOs, car-lenders, bullet-makers, bankers, and a thousand other similarly useless occupations. Business allows you not to hear the noise of time. So in order to keep busy, the industrious redirect time away from non-industrious activities: healing, educating, imagining, loving, sleeping.

Consequently, in an industrious society, teachers are not thought to educate their students about the marvelous disharmony of existence, but are reduced to the function of educators of industriousness. Doctors are not considered to be people who heal the body in order to make it capable of swimming or making love, but are humiliated in the role of repairers of perennially sick organisms, who are made capable, thanks to pharmacological maintenance, of performing economic functions.

Of course, the industrious consider themselves the salt of the earth, and despise the lazy idlers, because if it were up to those lazy people, we would never have made any progress, we would still be in the Stone Age. This is false, because idleness is the condition of all progress. Properly understood, technique is a cunning strategy of idleness.

Only a few decades ago (although it seems like millennia), the systematic application of idleness, combined with the systematic application of industriousness, reached an unstable point of equilibrium: thanks to Mediterranean workers' refusal to work, the Nordic masters had to hire engineers to invent devices apt to replace human labor. At that point, there was reason to hope that the industrious curse would come to an end: let's rest, travel, listen to music; let's all work very little, just the amount required to reproduce what is necessary.

But the worshipers of useless agitation, bitten by their atavistic sense of guilt, led by Mrs. Thatcher, restored order: they waged wars to destroy everything and then rebuild it, invented non-existent needs, organized society in such a way that freedom was called unemployment and everyone was forced to look for a job, however useless (or even absolutely harmful) in order to have a salary with which to buy those useless things that the industrious produce so as not to be deprived of the torment of doing, not to be forced to listen to the inner time that silently leads us to death. So we missed our appointment with happiness.

The outcome of that battle was predictable: there is no competition between a highly organized army of anxious, hyperactive fanatics and a multitude of idlers. The former will always win. Which proves the thesis that happiness is not a thing of this world.

So we are in hell, because we have missed the appointment (unique, unrepeatable, perhaps purely imaginary) that history had fixed for us with happiness.

Now, the most important question remains: Is it possible to live happily in hell? The answer can only be singular. And my singular answer is: Yes. How? I'm not telling you how, because I do not know. And also because he is wise who has seen a lot; he has forgotten nothing, yet he knows how to see everything as if it were for the first time.

Part 2

Desertion as Political Strategy

Questioning Depression

The tired no longer prepares for any possibility (subjective): he therefore cannot realize the smallest possibility (objective). But possibility remains, because you never realize all of the possible, you even bring it into being as you realize some of it. The tired has only exhausted realization, while the exhausted exhausts all of the possible. The tired can no longer realize, but the exhausted can no longer possibilitate. There is no more possibility: a relentless Spinozism. Does he exhaust the possible because he is himself exhausted, or is he exhausted because he has exhausted the possible? He exhausts himself in exhausting the possible, and vice versa. He exhausts that which is not realized through the possible.

Gilles Deleuze, "The Exhausted"[1]

Psycho-Energy Exhaustion

According to Deleuze and Guattari in *Anti-Oedipus*, desire is the tension that pushes and drags us towards an object that does not exist, but that we create precisely in the process of reaching for it. Far from being the satisfaction of a need, or the filling of a lack, desire is the creation of the other as attractor and projector. The object of desire is simultaneously attracting the subject, and also projecting the subject as other of the other.

It is in the realm of desire that the forces animating the social

---

1 Gilles Deleuze, "The Exhausted," trans. by Anthony Uhlman, *SubStance*, 24(3), Issue 78, (1995), p. 3.

sphere are born and set up. Since desire is the source of most radical complicity, the processes of historical subjectivation are driven by it. But the explosion and externalization of the unconscious that was provoked by the media machine in the era of global connection is causing a nervous breakdown of energy, triggering the pathological panic-depression cycle.

The semio-capitalist economy is ceaselessly spreading desire, but it postpones pleasure, because time must be invested in production, consumption, and competition.

Neoliberalism led to exasperation, a certain fanaticism of limitlessness that belongs to Western culture, particularly to the romantic legacy. In the twentieth century, the fanatical "no-limits" ideology of Marinetti's futurism exalted aggressiveness, violence, and war.

In the twenty-first century, this futuristic ideology has been revived by Californian biotechnological trans-humanism, a futurism of a senescent, hyper-techno society that has lost vital energy and aims to replace it with bio-electronic devices.

At a certain point in this psycho-cultural landscape there was a collapse: the explosion that was the pandemic coincided with a sudden, dramatic slowing of the social and psychic rhythm. I would call this "psycho-deflation," the deflation of the tension associated with desire, the sanitary interdiction of pleasure.

What imagination will be able to reactivate desire so that human evolution can escape the double spiral of chaos and automation, of war and techno-totalitarianism? Is a reactivation of psychological energy possible in a Western culture that is irreversibly decaying, and primarily for demographic reasons? Should we expect that Western culture will be able to deal with its own exhaustion (which is linked with the limits to economic growth)? Or should we expect that the white race will react to its own decline with suicidal aggression towards the whole of mankind? The latter is certainly possible, as the current inter-white war in Ukraine is suggesting.

It's not easy to say what depression is. It is not clear to the person who is depressed, who is unable to tell you exactly why she is depressed. But it's also not clear to the psychiatrist who diagnoses depression, and who doesn't exactly know what she's talking about.

At a certain point, the idea that depressive psychosis is the effect of some physical disturbance or neurological disfunction found traction and became hegemonic. Too little of this and too much of that ingredient, as if it were the recipe for soup. But the human mind is not soup. The brain can be compared to soup if you want, but the emotional mind is more complicated than the already hyper-complicated soup called the brain.

When one speaks of "the mind," they are not speaking of the mere dynamics of an organ, no matter how complex it is. One is rather speaking of life, of social interaction, of living time, of temporality as investment and loss. At the end one is speaking of death.

In the same year that Sándor Ferenczi wondered about the possibility of a therapy for mass psychosis, 1919, Yeats wrote these words:

> The best lack all conviction, while the worst
> Are full of passionate intensity.[2]

When the spark of collective imagination is extinguished, when the near-future appears unimaginable or fearful, when the best, as Yeats says, lack all energy and all conviction, then

---

2   William Butler Yeats, "The Second Coming."

the heroic spirit of passionate intensity, of nationalism and racism and hate, comes to the fore.

Then impotence turns into rancor, and those who have suffered humiliation proudly express the desire to humiliate others. All they can do, at that point, is be aggressive to those who are weaker. The Trump effect is all here: no Trumpist believes that Donald is a good person, a capable businessman, and an enlightened politician. I suspect they think the man is a psychopathic bastard. But it is precisely for this reason that they vote for him: because there is no one like him who can horrify the liberals and be responsible for their humiliation.

The Trump phenomenon has its roots in the frightening sadness of American life — the depression that is continuously obliged to turn into aggressive competition (like in the Sidney Pollack movie *They Kill Horses, Don't They?* (1969)).

We must interpret depression not only as a symptom, but as an agent of subjectivation. First of all we must remember that it is not only, and not even primarily, a pathology. It is also a form of knowledge. Hillman said that depression is the form of knowledge closest to the truth: the truth of the irreversibility of time, the truth of being in the horizon of death. Furthermore, we must try to understand how depression can evolve, on an individual and above all on a social level.

In *Black Sun*, published in 1987, Julia Kristeva writes:

Depressed persons do not defend themselves against death but against the anguish prompted by the erotic object. [...] Messengers of Thanatos, melancholy people are witness/accomplices of the signifier's flimsiness, the living being's precariousness.[3]

---

3 Julia Kristeva (1987) *Black Sun: Depression and Melancholia*, Columbia

Kristeva suggests that in the dynamics of depression there is a need to protect against frustration, which slows down desire, even to the point of stopping it entirely:

> Many models have been suggested in order to think out the processes underlying the depressive retardation state. One of them, "learned helplessness," is based on the following observation: when all escape routes are blocked, animals as well as men learn to withdraw rather than flee or fight. The retardation or inactivity, which one might call depressive, would thus constitute a learned defense reaction to a dead-end situation and unavoidable shocks.[4]

Should we really medicalize despair or sadness? Or should we accept the idea that in despair there is a painful awareness that we need to process something rather than remove it or bury it under an obligatory optimism?

It is obvious that we are sad when we realize that the life we have not asked to live is a cheat, that we'll work in precarious conditions for a shitty salary in order to barely survive, and that like Sisyphus, we'll be forever dragging a boulder that is becoming heavier and heavier every single day. We call it depression, but perhaps it is simply a matter of becoming aware.

Depression statistics are data about something we can't exactly define. By this I do not mean to imply that this data is meaningless — it shows that suffering grows as sociale pressure forces us to remove suffering in some way, with psychiatric drugs or with dullness, in order to be able to trust in deceitful promises. Let's call it what we want: depression,

---

University Press, p. 20.

4   *Ibid.*, p. 34.

sadness, or capitalism; what is certain is that these statistics mean something. What exactly?

The Prozac Years

In the 1990s, there was a lot of talk about neuroleptic or antipsychotic drugs, chemicals capable of regulating the traffic of neurotransmitters in such a way as to unblock something and circulate something else. Some of these drugs work well, or even very well, and sometimes they work very badly.

Certainly, so-called depressive states can be linked to biochemical phenomena such as the retention of dopamine by re-uptake inhibitors, and therefore it is useful in some cases to take drugs that antagonize the inhibitors, but this does not mean that we have explained the so-called depression phenomenon. According to Joanna Moncrieff, drug-centered psychopharmacology works (sometimes) because it produces positive effects regarding the symptoms of diseases such as depression. But this does not say much (or at least, not the essential thing) about those pathologies. To cite an example from Moncrieff, a moderate dose of alcohol can in some cases be used to overcome shyness and get closer to another person. But this does not mean that the person in question has an alcohol deficit which can be overcome with a glass of prosecco.[5]

According to Alberto Fernández Liria:

No specific genetic cause has been found for any mental disorder. [...] Furthermore, the frequency of mental disorders has not decreased, as has happened for diseases for which effective treatment has been found. While tuberculosis

---

5   Joanna Moncrieff (2013) *The Bitterest Pills: The Troubling Story of Antipsychotic Drugs*, Palgrave Macmillan.

practically disappeared when the specific treatment was discovered, mental disorders are apparently only increasing.[6]

Psychopharmacology perfects its techniques day by day, and often obtains important therapeutic results, but mental suffering does not stop expanding; or at least, an increasing number of people seem to be aware of their suffering and coming forward to declare it. Certainly, this may appear to be a disconfirmation of recent psycho-pharmacological findings, especially those based on the chemistry of neurotransmitters.

In the last decade of the twentieth century, I read a fashionable book about a very, very fashionable pill: Prozac.[7] Those were the years when the liberal mono-culture was establishing itself, in which workers were forced to be free agents or self-entrepreneurs so that they could be exploited to the limit of exhaustion and set against each other in a self-defeating competition whose effect was to lower wages and so on. We know that story, and we know where it has led us, even if we may not know it fully yet.

I re-read that book, Peter Kramer's *Listening to Prozac*, and realized that, regardless of any judgment of therapeutic efficacy, the depression Kramer talks about is nothing more than the pain caused by hyper-competitive stress. A pill was needed so that those who did not manage to become wicked machines could silence suffering, discomfort, and their disgust at themselves. The result is that during the 1990s, many people became wicked, cynical machines, and those who did not succeed in this, entered a stable state of depression, with or without

6   Alberto Fernández Liria, "El fiasco de la psiquiatría "biológica," *CTXT*, August 2022.

7   Peter Kramer (1998) *Listening to Prozac: The Landmark Book About Antidepressants and the Remaking of the Self*, Penguin.

suicide. I'm talking here about the generation of Mark Fisher, the thinker who more than any other was able to describe the socio-cultural genesis of depression from the inside.

While largely dedicated to extolling the amazing therapeutic effects of Prozac, Kramer's book is problematically constructed, in the sense that the author wonders if the psychiatrist, who should allow the patient to recover his psycho-physical integrity, has the right to transform his patient, to reprogram his reactivity and behavior through the chemical modification of his brain. Of course, this is a question full of psychological and philosophical implications. What does it mean to "be oneself"? What is "the self"? Can we speak of an individual's psychological identity without taking into account the fact that that identity is formed through a series of existential and social events, and also through their relationship with food, drugs, and so on? But the point that interests me most in the book is the model of normalcy that Kramer claims he wants to restore by administering Prozac.

The patients Kramer talks about (Tess, Julia, Lucy) are women who cannot keep up with the pace of their increasingly stressful, physically and psychologically tiring lives: they are mothers, wives, and workers in a context that values only the winners, the competitive ones. In these cases, says Kramer, Prozac works; maybe not always, but mostly. That is, it allows patients to take care of their husbands' children and work at the office with more diligence than before, and moreover to smile in humiliating situations, or to confront unflinchingly the union representatives who are asking for a salary increase for their workers. It allows them to be winners, to be able to hide from themselves the abyss that winning brings about.

In the 1990s, Prozac removed from conscious vision what was brewing in American society, and what since 11 September

2001 has become unconcealable: the American abyss whose depth we are measuring and whose consequences we cannot at present foresee.

From these reflections, I draw the provisional conclusion that when we talk about depression, we are talking about a vast (infinite) palette of painful feelings that can largely be traced back to the perception of oneself in social interaction. I do not exclude the possibility that there are organic causes that favor sadness, and that there are substances that can chemically cure psychic pain, but sadness is not a disease, especially if we are talking about people who have to do lifelong jobs that are poorly paid and devoid of sense — the great majority of the population. And if the future that lies ahead is an interminable continuation of this condition of precariousness and stressful senselessness, sadness is inevitable, especially if you have introjected the idea that you are responsible, and that if you want you can get what you want, (a better salary or the end of climate change) it is to some extent your fault.

The disease is not depression, the disease is capitalism, as I read on a wall of a district in Santiago de Chile. I wonder: What if we get rid of the idea that we are responsible for what happens to us and to others? the idea that if we try our best, we can do it? and that we must have a recognized identity? What if we minimize our economic needs, reducing to a minimum our compulsory social interactions?

I leave this question pending, but I intend to return to this subject in a while.

The Third Unconscious

The philosopher may perhaps say that depression is a condition of dangerous proximity to the ultimate truth, the one that should not be seen, like the face of Medusa. The philosopher may perhaps reveal that the main reason it is worth living philosophically is precisely this: philosophical thought makes it possible to see the face of Medusa without being paralyzed and annihilated by it.

But since it is not easy for anyone (not even philosophers) to live philosophically, we must recognize that depression comes as a paralysis of our imagination of the future, as a decrease in desire, which results in a weakening, or even a zeroing out, our attraction to reality.

What we do know is that more and more people are being diagnosed with depression, to the point that depression is considered to be the most common pathology among young people. I suspect that, today, this nosological category is used to refer to something that can no longer be identified with tormenting melancholy or with the sense of failure. We call it "depression," but we are actually facing something the meaning and dynamics of which are more and more elusive. Certainly depression is rampant; however, this is not really depression per se, but something else that we call by the name "depression" for want of another word, lack of another concept more appropriate to the existential and psychic modality that is emerging.

In the last century, other pathologies competed for primacy: in the bourgeois era, when Freud founded a discipline designed to make comprehensible the dynamics of the unconscious, neurosis enjoyed (so to speak) this primacy, as a pathology indissociable from civilization. The repression of sexual desire, the moral and social obligation to live in conditions that repressed the erotic drive, induced neurotic reactions in subjects who were unable to compensate for the frustration of the libido with so-called superior sublimating activities.

Then, in the last part of the twentieth century, the psychic dynamics changed, and libidinal repression was replaced by a sort of unleashing of the desiring energies in conditions of competition and constant acceleration of the psycho-stimulatory machine of globalized media. For a certain period of time, schizophrenia took centre stage in the attention of psychiatrists and seemed to spread as a pathology and also as an existential style.

"Just do it" was then the symbol of a lifestyle, of a passage towards the act without reflection. Neoliberalism, which considers economic profit the only value worthy of being considered, triggered schizoid-type processes and caused a sort of explosion of the unconscious, externalized in the phantasmagoria of commodity images.

The third decade of the twenty-first century opened with a collapse of the energy hyper-stimulated by schizo-pathogenic neoliberalism: psycho-deflation first spread as a consequence of a virus, but then ended up settling at the heart of the hyper-stimulated collective organism.

The question I ask myself is: How does social subjectivity evolve in the conditions of depressive collapse that are manifesting? Haven't we entered a psychosphere within which the collective unconscious takes on a different rhythm?

Psycho-Deflation and the Social Dimension of Depression

The collective reaction that followed the viral trauma and pandemic psycho-deflation has taken on a psychotic feature since February 2022.

Now we are facing again the question that Sándor Ferenczi asked himself in 1919: Can we treat mass psychosis? How does social subjectivity evolve in these conditions of depressive collapse?

Epidemic depression is a condition that leads many people to bunch up and turn aggressive in the herd. This is a description of the genesis of fascism. Although Ferenczi could not answer his own question, in the decade following 1919 the cure was found by warmongering dictators. One hundred years later, we find ourselves in a situation similar to Ferenczi's.

At this point, a leader emerges who promises the humiliation of those who have imposed humiliation upon us, and the masses follow him, until the next defeat. We must interpret depression not only as a symptom, but as an agent of subjectivation. Freud, in a note to *Civilization and its Discontents*, wrote: "One day someone will venture to embark upon a pathology of cultural communities."[8] That day is now.

The idea that psychotherapy should go beyond the individual dimension of Freudian psychoanalysis is not new. In *Collective Consciousness and Cultural Healing*, Duane Elgin retraces the awakening of collective consciousness in the works of Carl Gustav Jung, Erich Neumann, and Ken Wilber.[9] Many therapists, particularly in Latin America, have followed the path of group therapy, based on the theory that the link ("*vinculo*," in the words of the Swiss-Argentinian Pichon-Rivière) is a dynamic relation of reciprocal change that must be interpreted and cured within groups of reciprocal analysis. Group therapy has developed as a useful methodology for the understanding and cure of psychotic individuals. But we have to go beyond group therapy, and we must interpret mental suffering from the point of view of a social genealogy of the symptom.

Nevertheless, we lack a theory of the genealogy of mass

---

8   Freud, *Civilization and its Discontents*.
9   Duane Elgin (1997) *Collective Consciousness and Cultural Healing*, Millennium Project.

psychosis, and *a fortiori*, we lack a therapeutic approach to this kind of disease. I am not speaking here of group therapy of individual disease: I'm talking of something different — a condition of widely shared pathology.

Recently, because of the worldwide contagion of Covid-19, epidemiology has come to the center of the scientific stage. We should approach the psycho-cultural phenomenon that is shortly labeled "fascism" as an object of reflection for epidemiologists. Psycho-epidemiology should become a special branch of clinical discourse, as well as the most important branch of political discourse.

Disinvestment of Desire

If we consider depression as a form of knowledge, we can develop this sentiment from the inside. What we need is not a denial of the contents of depression, nor the mere removal of the suffering that depression entails, but awareness of the meaning of the message that depression conveys. Depression carries a message, and we should start by recognizing its cognitive value, in order to get free from the effects of isolation, loneliness, and despair, and in order to reactivate the imagination based on the acceptance of depression's message, not on its denial.

It is the ambiguousness of psycho-deflation that interests me, because this ambiguity can evolve in a manner that does not deny the contents of depression, but turns those contents into collective realizations, tenderness, and relaxation.

From my point of view, the message that we may disentangle from depressive symptoms concerns desertion: desertion from war, desertion from nationalism, but also from the expectation of a better future, a future of expansion, of accumulation. Interpreting depression is a philosophical, psychoanalytic, and political task. In my opinion, it is the main task we have to face today.

In 1998, Alain Ehrenberg published *Weariness of the Self: Diagnosing the History of Depression in the Contemporary Age*. Ehrenberg captures the essential core of that form of suffering that was spreading in the years of neoliberal revolution: in his view, depression is intimately linked to competition and a sense of failure, of inadequacy. "The depressed individual is unable to measure up; he is tired of having to become himself."[10]

Speaking of the cult of business that has emerged since the 1980s, he says that:

the business environment is the antechamber of the nervous breakdown [...] The means of regulating and dominating the workforce were based less on blind obedience and more on initiative: responsibility, ability to evolve and create projects, motivation, flexibility, and so on They are not trying to make the body submissive; they are hoping to mobilize the affect and mental capacities of each employee."[11]

The neoliberal decades have subjected nervous energies to constant stress, and have produced effects of psychic fatigue that have taken the clinical form of depression. All this was very interesting and useful in those years, but perhaps today we have to read depression in a different way, no longer as a failure of libidinal investments, but as conscious disinvestment. As resignation. From this point on, I will

---

10 Alain Ehrenberg (2016) *Weariness of the Self: Diagnosing the History of Depression in the Contemporary Age*, McGill-Queen's University Press, p. 4.

11 *Ibid.*, p. 184.

develop my philosophical project by deepening the meaning of resignation.

Hikikomori

In the winter of 2007, I met a young Japanese intellectual named Kazuki Sagurada, who allowed me to understand something that comes back to my mind today. At that point, his words sounded to me like an illumination.

Kazuki told me about a phenomenon that was spreading in his country: a million young Japanese people, mostly males, were locking themselves inside their homes, interrupting all social relationships for months or years, or even for a lifetime. They only opened their bedroom door to receive the food they needed for survival, and used their Internet connection as their only window to the world. These metropolitan hermits were called (and still are, because the phenomenon is far from over and has not stopped spreading) "hikikomori."

When Kazuki told about this social phenomenon, I reacted with consternation, commenting that it seemed to me a state of extreme alienation. But Kazuki expressed his disagreement, and surprised me by saying that he too had been a hikikomori for a couple of years, and that only by reading the writings of Félix Guattari and the theorists of Italian autonomy did he come to understand that the hikikomori were brothers of the autonomous Europeans, because like them they wanted to interrupt their relationship with an intolerable society.

If you have some hint of daily life in a Japanese city, then you will understand that the only psychically healthy people are those who no longer want to have any relationship with work, consumption, the subway at seven in the morning, and the continuous relationship tension between people who are all equally stressed. Kazuki told me that the condition of hikikomori had allowed him to create a space for living and an autonomous awareness.

Since then, I have begun to think that the suspension of desire may have another explanation than the depression to which we usually attribute it. It may instead be a conscious desertion of the infernal society that is the product of decades of competitive acceleration.

Another Japanese friend who has influenced me in recent years is Sabu Kohso, a writer who lives between New York and Tokyo and who has published a book called *Radiation and Revolution*, dedicated to the political and theoretical consequences of the Fukushima event. The lesson that Sabu draws from that event is that we live in a phase of divergence between the history of the world and the evolution of the earth:

> Today, the material limit of the World, whose expansion is driven by capital's critical reproduction, is exposed more catastrophically than ever. [...] The Fukushima event [...] materializes the breach of World History and all its progressivist promises, through which full experiences of life and death on Earth are surfacing. This is dreadful, but it is necessary for action.[12]

The materiality of the planet — water, air, and fire — erupts through the cracks of the history of the world, shattering the network of abstractions that have supported that history up to now: the abstraction of economic value, of political law, of values, ideals, and morals.

Starting from this crumbling, we must rethink the psycho-political problem of depression as a *creative resignation* in the

---

12 Sabu Kohso (2020) *Radiation and Revolution*, Duke University Press, pp. 8–9.

face of the collapse of all values (economic and ideological) that previously acted as effective motivations to action in modern centuries. Starting from this sinking, we must imagine.

An imagination of the unimaginable is the psycho-political cure we are looking for in this phase of psycho-deflation and the chaos that follows. It is a question of interpreting depression as being in harmony with the exhaustion of the physical and nervous resources that made the history of civilization possible. As long as we are unable to think about exhaustion, as long as we are unable to imagine from the point of view of exhaustion, we will be exposed to these storms of murderous dementia: wars, fascisms, and mass suicide.

Daily experience seems to confirm the perception of a widespread depression — *seems to*, but is it true? What if those symptoms (a reduced propensity for socialization, little availability to enterprise, anxiety about the future and impotence) are signs of a different disorder, one that might not even *be* a disorder, but a pathway to a different cure?

They say that the depressed individual tends to avoid sociality. But what sociality are we speaking of? The sociality of the employment office? The sociality of competition propelled by advertising and Instagram? The military mobilization of existence? Or the defense of our sacred homeland?

Evolution of the Depressive Context
In his book *Le ragioni del dolore* (*The Reasons for Pain*), Piero Coppo emphasizes the link between depression and a sense of guilt:

> Melancholy, inherent in the human condition after the expulsion from Eden, means the loss of direct contact with the divine. Christian moral theology amplified the sense of guilt

and unworthiness that certainly did not initially constitute the main character of melancholy.[13]

Of course, Protestantism further amplified the blame for the melancholy, and the melancholic person is furthermore reproached for not having the energy necessary to carry out the tasks which God and the community have assigned him.

In the contemporary mental condition of the very young, however, it does not seem to me that blame plays an important role, so I'm not sure if this definition of depression captures the specificity of the mental suffering of the most depressed generation of all time. Emotional distancing appears to be much more relevant than culpability.

What is certain is that the generation that has learned more words from machines than from their mothers suffers at the same time from neuro-informational overstimulation and from contact deprivation. Therefore we can talk about psychopathies of anxiety and panic, and we can see some tendencies towards normalization of autistic behavior. But the diagnosis of depression does not grasp the novelty of a pathology that manifests itself not so much as blame, but as emotional distancing.

That diagnosis captures an analogy with the discomfort of previous generations — for example, the generation that suffered the impact of the digital transformation of liberal culture when it was already in adulthood, when it had formed its unconscious and rational expectations.

Perhaps we must begin to distinguish between the behavior of the first connective generation — marked by desocialization — and that of the previous generation (Mark Fisher's). As I've

---

13 Piero Coppo (2005) *Le ragioni del dolore. Etnopsichiatria della depression*, Bollati Boringhieri.

already said, Fisher describes very well the depression resulting from competitive failure that Ehrenburg was already discussing at the end of the 1980s. His generation, in fact, believed to some extent in the promises of democracy and globalization before experiencing the excitement of acceleration, and before realizing they were trapped in a dead end.

The "last generation," however, does not seem to be suffering from their deprivation, from the sense of failure, or the absence of choice. It seems to me that, for this generation, there is no failure, as they have given up the race before starting it. It is as if the connective generation already know there is nothing to be done. Therefore, there is no guilt in doing nothing.

"When the Crab Realizes That There Is No Seagull"

Psychic desertion — the refusal to participate in the game of war, which is swallowing, little by little, every other game.

It seems to me that the "last generation" sees that the expectations (affective, working, and political) developed over the last five hundred years are traps into which it would be stupid to fall again. I am not speaking of consciousness, but of perception; an ambiguous, indefinite perception which can evolve in the direction of a new awareness, a new paradigm of existence and social production, or sink into a rancorous, aggressive nihilism, like fascism.

Fascism today is an obligatory mobilization of energies that we have no desire to mobilize. Think of the campaign aimed to increase births. It is highly probable that living in the future will be horrible. Not certain, but likely. Why should we make children? Why should we hand over innocent people to the killing machines of war, climatic apocalypse, and increasingly brutal labor exploitation? Why should we contribute to overpopulation in conditions of water scarcity? Having children means putting yourself in a condition of dependence on a society with which we no longer have reason to identify, and with whose continuation we do not intend to collaborate in any way.

There is no reason to mobilize our psychic energies for a world that has already completed its lifecycle and which survives only by sucking the psychic and economic blood of those who still fall for it:

> A commonly used test: over a crab in a basin a white sheet is repeatedly passed. The wavering sheet is perceived by the crab as a seagull, his natural predator. How long does it stir, running everywhere in the basin in search of a shelter that is not there, before remaining motionless, giving up all attempts? Here despair is literally understood as a loss of hope that motivates the action. When all available means have been put in place to get out of an unbearable and dangerous situation to no avail, the crab rests, to save what's left of his energy.[14]

I believe that in the mind's evolution, we have finally reached the point when inactivity is more brainy (and more ethical) than activity. The generation that was born after the turn of the century are probably learning this lesson, and will no longer act out of fear of the frightening shadows moving over their heads.

Resignation is a better starting point than seeking therapy for a depression that does not resemble to what we used to call depression in the past.

We are continually told that we must not be overcome by

---

14 Coppo, *Le ragioni del dolore*, pp. 69–70.

despair and that we must return to battle. They break our ears with the exhortation to courage, to enterprise. What should we undertake, and why? We know that the battle they urge us to fight will end badly, like all previous ones.

Previous generations have allowed themselves to be persuaded, and have continually started running again. This new generation of humans has planned to be the last. They call themselves the "last generation" not out of self-pity or with any plaintive intention, but rather as an affirmation, a claim: Since there is no longer any possibility of a future that is not horrible, we have decided to be the last, as the crab in the basin has decided not to struggle anymore to run from a machine that is terrifying and killing him.

Resign

Indignation?

Time for Outrage! is the title of a book by Stephane Hessel that was widely read in the years of the Occupy movement, just after the financial crisis of 2008, when millions of people worldwide protested against the arrogance of the financial class and the the impoverishment of society.

Lots of people were indignant and marched in the streets of New York, Athens, Cairo, London, and many other cities, but financial automaton prevailed, and the rationale of the financial algorithm forced workers to bend to the law of profit. Democracy entered the final phase of its agony, which reached its climax in summer 2015.

That summer was the climactic moment of indignation, but also of impotence: 62 percent of voters said no to the financial injunctions and to the blackmail of the European Central Bank, however, two days after the referendum, Alexis Tsipras went to Brussels to accept the memorandum that Greek citizens had just rejected. At that point, we realized that democracy was extinguished in exactly the place where twenty-five centuries ago it had been invented.

Since then, we have not stopped being outraged, but impotent indignation is bad for our health. And our social health, and particularly our mental health, has gotten worse and worse.

I know that it's not possible to get rid of anger with a gesture of will, but it is useful to know that for decades the mental equilibrium of the population has been eroded by a combination of indignation at the intolerable and the inexorability of the impoverishment and humiliation prescribed by the logic of financial algorithms.

Since the will can do nothing against a system of abstract automatisms, it is useful to process anger in a way that externalizes it and makes it independent from any social bond: this is desertion. This is the method that should be adopted once we realize the powerlessness of political will and the irreversibility of catastrophe.

For decades, humiliation and helpless anger have fueled a psychotic epidemic accompanied by the massive spread of opiates and other addictive psychopharmacological substances. Then Covid-19 broke out, and the West found itself swaying on the edge of mental collapse.

In the United States, the number of overdose deaths from synthetic opioids such as fentanyl and oxycontin has exceeded the number of deaths from firearms (which are not few in that country), and even the number of deaths in road accidents. In 2020 there were one hundred thousand deaths from opioid overdoses, sixty-two-thousand of which were caused by Fentanyl alone, a pain-relieving pill widely recommended by doctors to the great profit of Big Pharma shareholders.[1] We should therefore ask ourselves if indignation (an immediate reaction to the intolerable) is the appropriate key with which to free ourselves from the intolerable, and whether perhaps we should conclude that, from an evolutionary point of view, it is time to resign ourselves to the end of the modern illusion of political democracy and economic growth.

---

1 Centers for Disease Control and Prevention (2001) "Drug Overdose Deaths in the U.S. Top 100,000 Annually," https://www.cdc.gov/nchs/pressroom/nchs_press_releases/2021/20211117.htm

But we also must resign ourselves to the impotence of human will, and therefore of politics, the source of delusion and frustration.

Liberal democracy has been strategically defeated because it believed that reason and law could hold off the aggressive instincts of capitalism and the reactions that follow impoverishment and panic, which, finding no political outcome, end up fueling neo-reactionary movements.

We must abandon a horizon so that another horizon can reveal itself.

The horizon of the third decade of the twenty-first century is darker than ever, assuming that the old metaphor of light and dark retains some of its evocative power. It is dark because we have realized that reason can no longer rule the world, if it ever did, and technology, although very powerful, can do nothing against time and death, and can do little against chaos.

In *Dialectic of Enlightenment*, published in 1944, Horkheimer and Adorno grasped, albeit with their Hegelian language, the core of the barbarism they had witnessed helplessly:

We have no doubt — and herein lies our *petitio principii* — that freedom in society is inseparable from enlightenment thinking. We believe we have perceived with equal clarity, however, that the very concept of that thinking, no less than the concrete historical forms, the institutions of society with which it is intertwined, already contains the germ of the regression which is taking place everywhere today. If enlightenment does not assimilate reflection on this regressive moment, it seals its own fate. By leaving consideration of the destructive side of progress to its enemies, thought in its headlong rush into pragmatism is forfeiting its sublating character, and therefore its relation to truth.[2]

As neoliberalism began to produce its effects of precariousness, super-exploitation, and extreme loneliness, a neo-reactionary movement grew on a global scale, corroding liberal democracy, but at the same time allying with predatory corporate liberalism. This global neo-reactionary movement, composed of a patchwork of irreconcilable particularisms, contends with liberal democracy for world domination. But this conflict between the free world and an assortment of identity claims does not appear to be in any way resolvable, and it is taking place against the backdrop of nuclear proliferation.

Now we understand the meaning of the prophecy of Günther Anders, who after Hiroshima, and in the era of nuclear proliferation, predicted a return of Nazism:

> We can expect that the horrors of the Reich to come will vastly eclipse the horrors of yesterday's Reich. Doubtless, when one day our children or grandchildren, proud of their perfect "co-mechanization," look down from the great heights of their thousand-year Reich at yesterday's empire, at the so-called "third" Reich, it will seem to them merely a minor, provincial experiment...[3]

---

2 Max Horkheimer and Theodor Adorno (2002) *Dialectic of Enlightenment: Philosophical Fragments*, trans. by Edmund Jephcott, Stanford University Press, p. xvi.

3 Günther Anders (2003) *Die Atomare Drohung: Radikale Überlegungen zum atomaren Zeitalter*, Taschenbuch, p. 93.

The Long Covid of the Social Mind

In the last pages of *The Plague*, Camus recounts the joyful return to life of the city of Oran after the end of the epidemic. Two years after the virus outbreak, after three campaigns of vaccination, no signs of an upcoming joyfulness can be detected. On the contrary, it seems that the signs of a psycho-social unease are deepening. Apart from the medical consideration of the virus's persistence, I am interested in thinking about a kind of "Long Covid of the social mind."

Long Covid is defined as a prolonged persistence of symptoms of various kinds after contagion and recovery. A friend who suffered from it told me that the main symptom for her was constant exhaustion, a loss of energy, and even some mental confusion, which some call brain fog. Exhaustion and mental confusion seem to dominate the contemporary scene.

The economic, geopolitical, and mental chaos that the virus has produced seem to persist, and indeed increase, exceeding the positive effects of mass vaccination. The virus acted as a catalyst for opposing ghosts: paranoid ghosts of conspiracy and hypochondriacal ghosts of fear.

Subjectivity and public discourse have been invaded by paradoxical alternatives and double binds. This sanitary injunction caused mixed reactions: denial and phobia.

Even if everybody admits that the weakness of public health institutions has paved the way for the severity of epidemics, governments have profited from the state of emergency in terms of further privatization and the precaritization of labor. For the plunderers, the emergency must not end, and the media must not stop the panic campaign that has engulfed the collective discourse for a year and a half.

For two years we have been exposed to a flow of panicking

images: nurses with green robes, sanitary masks, protective attires, ambulances, syringes of different dimensions, and most of all, injections, hundreds of injections from morning to night, with the predictable effect of feeding panic and pushing the population to obey all kinds of orders. The social body is caught in a crisis of interminable hypochondria: fear of giving up fear.

In August 2021, Joe Biden announced the end of war in Afghanistan. One thing has been particularly impressive to me in the Western defeat: the mental mayhem. Biden had said weeks before that we would not again see scenes like those at the Saigon embassy in 1975. Actually, we have seen scenes much worse: the panic of the crowd at the airport, the massacre of more or less innocent people. In those frantic days, Americans left behind thousands of collaborators and betrayed the expectations of millions of women who made the mistake of believing that Western people are omnipotent. Everybody in the world was led to acknowledge that Western people are traitors and cowards. August 2021 was the moment when the disintegration of Western civilization was exposed worldwide.

Not only arrogance, not only bumptiousness, but blatant incompetence: this is the spectacle that the leaders of the free world presented in those days. However, we must see that, beyond incompetence, the problem is mental mayhem, a state of mental confusion.

When I saw poor Biden after the terrorist attack that murdered two hundred people in Kabul Airport, including thirteen American soldiers and three British citizens, I had the impression he was babbling nonsensical words. Mental mayhem. This is what happens to Western people in general.

Panic is the effect of being exposed to a level of complexity that exceeds our mental capacity to elaborate it, and of facing a sequence of non-decidable alternatives: chaos. The social mind has grown unable to process information and to govern the surrounding world.

Panic is the mental and behavioral manifestation of an organism that is overwhelmed by the flow of non-governable events. Here we are: the erosion of the environment, multiplication of conflicts, and acceleration of info-neural stimuli have obliterated our ability to decide. The more we know, the less we understand. The more we know, the more we face the alternatives: panic or depression. Frantic mobilization or despondency and passivity.

Is there a political therapy for panic? I don't think so, as panic is the deactivation of the political mind. Is there a psychoanalytic therapy for collective panic? This is the question that Ferenczi could not answer one hundred years ago.

Prescribing the Symptom

Indeed, the usual therapeutic techniques do not seem to work in large-scale catastrophe scenarios. The suffering of individuals can be cured, but we do not know how to cure collective panic, so the crowds go mad looking for an enemy, and find him in the poorest, the weakest, the most defenseless: Jews in Hitler's Germany, Muslims in Narendra Modi's India, refugees in von der Leyen's Europe.

Big Pharma has been exploiting this psychotic-depressive epidemic for many years, cashing in fabulous sums with the massive distribution of opiates, and scientific research is oriented towards chemical therapies that act on the individual without being able to scratch the collective roots of pain and panic in the slightest.

But the social organism can autonomously develop adaptive therapy strategies. Panic can have a function, as in the case of the flying sentries of some bird species when exposed to predators: the clamoring sentries trigger what appears to be a disordered reaction in the flock, but it has considerable defensive effectiveness as it confuses and frustrates the attacker's tactics. Depression can have the function of lessening a painful tension so as to slowly bring one out of the pathogenic whirlwind of info-stimulation.

I wonder if it would not be appropriate to think in paradoxical terms, as some authors suggest we do, in evidently desperate situations.

Resignation sounds anathema since modernity has mobilized all social energies in order to achieve the objectives of growth, progress, and accumulation of capital, all presented as the only salvation, the only eternity that is granted to humans after the disappearance of God. It would be useful to elaborate on the meaning of this word in order to discover its paradoxical healing power and its liberating political potential.

First of all, resignation means the recognition of something inevitable (like death), and it can act as an antidote to panic. In a situation of irreversible deterioration of the planetary environment, it can be assumed that the only salvation from extinction consists precisely in a general lowering of tension: a generalized psycho-inflation can cause a reduction in all consumption, first of all of energy consumption.

Causing a reduction in the consumption of energy and emission of pollutants, the lockdown made possible an involuntary decompression, with ambivalent effects, including tiredness, melancholy, and loneliness, but also the intuition of a different rhythm of life, one without stress or obligations. This slowdown exposed the possibility of a withdrawal. There was no need for acceleration, no need for accumulation, no need for useless things to consume.

A new space is presently opening to psychoanalysis, since politics can do nothing: a space for paradoxical therapy, based on the prescription of the symptom that Paul Watzlawick talks about in *Pragmatics of Human Communication*. If the symptom is impotence, and impotence is leading to depression, let's accept impotence as a condition and relax.

For Christians, resignation to the will of God is a virtue. As I don't believe in the will of God, I do not think that resignation is a virtue, but instead a therapy and redefinition of the field of world expectations constituting the discovery of another horizon. Resignation is not only a surrender, it is also a re-signification, because it gives new meaning to the signs of which social life is composed. A movement of surrender (of work, of consumption, of dependence) would remove all energy from the accumulation machine. It is illusory to think that in the post-pandemic future a revolution, a democratic redemption of some kind, could take place. The collective organism is weakened physically and psychically; depression is rampant. However, this weakness can be an invincible weapon if we learn how to use it strategically and transform it into widespread consciousness.

Let's reset social energy and abandon work and consumption. Mass defeatism, desertion, and sabotage — let these be our weapons in the time to come.

There is no political way out of the apocalypse. The left has been the main political instrument of the ultra-capitalist offensive for thirty years — anyone who invests their hopes in the left deserves to be betrayed, since betrayal is the only activity the left is capable of competently performing. The left's movements have been liquefied by panic-depressive psychosis. Subjectivity is at the mercy of psychosis, socially fractured.

The only possibility left to us is a paradoxical strategy that transforms psycho-deflation into a wave of slowing down, of blocking, of silencing, of shutting down the machine.

Depression is a symptom of political powerlessness and existential loneliness. Sometimes prescribing the symptom, as suggested by Watzlawick, can be the way to end suffering and change the pathogenic context.

The Unthinkable

The Collapse of the Western Mind

We are in the middle of the rapid disintegration of the geopolitical order inherited from the history of modern colonialism: the core of this disintegration, however, is the mental collapse of the Western world.

The legacy of five centuries of white colonization of the world is crumbling, and the white, senescent dominators are unable to hold the world of their own making together, so they accelerate the spread of violence.

The viral storm of Covid-19 has provoked a wave of chaos far beyond the sanitary sphere, as the virus is an unpredictable and undecidable factor bringing about environmental chaos, social chaos, mental chaos, and last but not least, geopolitical chaos. When the viral black swan started squawking under the guise of a viral storm, many other black swans awoke and started squawking together in a cacophonic concert.

The Unthinkable

Unthinkable is the title of Jamie Raskin's book published on the first anniversary of the strange insurrection that brought thousands of Trumpists into the political heart of the US.

Raskin is not just any writer — he is an important member of the US Congress, elected by the Maryland constituency, in the ranks of Democratic Party. Furthermore, he is a professor of constitutional law, a self-proclaimed liberal, and the father of three young persons in their twenties. One of them,

Tommy, twenty-five years old — a political activist, supporter of progressive causes, and a compassionate, empathic young man — died on the last day of the year 2020. To be more precise, Tommy committed suicide as the result of long-lasting depression and (it goes without saying) the long moral humiliation of his humanitarian values.

The suicide of his beloved son was an apocalypse in the mind of Jamie Raskin, for whom Tommy's final decision was not only an affective catastrophe, but the trigger of a radical re-consideration of his political beliefs.

Reading *Unthinkable*, I shared the pain of a father and the torment of an intellectual, while simultaneously being led to consider the depth of the crisis that is tearing apart Western culture and particularly the horizon of liberal democracy.

The book assembles three different stories that are deployed simultaneously and which feed into each other in many ways. The first is about American fascism, presenting the Trump administration as a kingdom of ignorance, racism, and aggressiveness. The second is about Tommy, his formation, his ideals, and the constant humiliation of his ethical sensibility. The third is about the effect of Covid-19 on the minds of the young generation that suffered most from social distancing, looming depression, and the inability to imagine a livable future. Tommy had been suffering from depression, as he mentioned in his final message: "Please forgive me, my illness won today." The note goes on: "Look after each other, the animals, and the global poor for me."[1]

Raskin has always considered himself "an optimist" and "radically optimistic about how the Constitution of the nation

---

1   Jamie Raskin (2022) *Unthinkable: Trauma, Truth, and the Trials of American Democracy*, Harper, p. 3.

itself can uplift our social, political, and intellectual condition."[2] After the death of his son, however, his self-perception changed. His constitutional optimism was shattered by the prevailing of brutality over the force of reason, and by the spread of depression:

> Suddenly, this constitutional optimism shames and embarrasses me.
>
> I fear that my sunny political optimism, what many of my friends have treasured in me most, has become a trap for massive self-delusion, a weakness to be exploited by our enemies. Yet I am also terrified to think about what it would mean to live without this buoyancy — and also without my beloved, irreplaceable son. The two always went hand-in-hand, and now I may be alive on earth without either of them.[3]

The political optimism of this generous law professor was shaken by the sudden realization that liberal democracy rests on a fragile foundation. In fact, he writes, "seven of our first ten presidents were slave owners. These facts are not accidental but arise from the very architecture of our political institutions."[4]

Slavery is part of the psychic baggage of the American nation. How can this nation claim to be seen as an example to others? How can we avoid thinking that this nation is a danger to the survival of humanity?

---

2   *Ibid.*, p. 15.
3   *Ibid.*
4   *Ibid.*, p. 87.

The Unthinkable Disintegration of the Monster

In the speech that Biden gave on 6 January 2022, one year after the Trumpist insurrection, he said: "We must decide what kind of nation we want to be."

Can America decide that violence is not the norm if American history is based on violence, slavery, and genocide?

The irredeemableness of that past is a source of systemic depression for the West, and therefore a systemic source of fascism, at least while we fail to devise a successful therapeutic strategy, a treatment for depression that acts strategically to free the energy of society from the trap of capitalism.

This is the point, on a theoretical level: Can we predict the outcome of a wave of social depression? Can we act on the evolution of the psychotic epidemic that we have been experiencing powerlessly for years?

Past experience teaches us that one way to react to depression is fascism, which transforms depression into violence against a ghostly enemy. This depression-fascism cycle has been reactivated in every part of the world, and especially in the United States. What is the alternative? For Tommy Raskin, the alternative was death.

How can we divert the trajectory of depression towards re-signification? Is resignation an option?

The word "resignation" resonates in my mind like a puzzle. For most people, resignation means quitting your job; another meaning is the acceptance of destiny, bowing one's head, submitting to the will of an almighty yet sometimes evil God. I, however, suggest a third meaning: re-signifying social life, changing the horizon of expectations, focusing frugally on profit rather than on the abstract value of money, on pleasure rather than accumulation, and on solidarity rather than competition. Delivering a similar psycho-cultural change out of the viral storm is the intellectual task of the present.

Reading Raskin's book confirmed my belief that the United States as a political entity is on the edge of an abyss, one that is inscribed in the history of that country.

In the decades following World War II, the United States succeeded in an unprecedented miracle: it lost almost all the wars in which it engaged — starting with the war in Vietnam and leading up to that in Afghanistan — without losing its global hegemony. In fact, this hegemony is based on two pillars: The first is certainly the US's absolute military prevalence, which is divided into a decentralized system of bases that cover a large part of the globe and make the North American territory inaccessible to military attacks by any other power. The second is the strength of its market economy, which reached the peak of its ability to penetrate and dominate when all the obstacles to globalization were removed — that is, after the collapse of Soviet socialism.

After 11 September 2001, one of these pillars began to fail. For the first time, a major military attack was conducted in the heart of American territory. We can regard Osama bin Laden as an obscurantist authoritarian killer, no doubt, but we cannot deny the strategic genius of the one who carried out the most effective war action of all time, pushing the giant into the self-destructive madness that manifested itself during Bush's presidency.

In the meantime, a decisive event has occurred: the technology necessary for the production of the atomic bomb has spread, and is now within the reach of a dozen countries, some of which are governed by characters whose behavior is difficult to predict. With this, the balance of terror that guaranteed the United States' hegemony has blown apart, along with the theory of mutually-assured destruction, which was based on the symmetrical positioning of two nuclear actors.

But the dynamic has also changed with regard to the indisputable strength of the market economy, which imposed US hegemony even after sensational defeats like the one in Vietnam. The global hegemony of the market has been jeopardized by Trump, in perfect harmony with Putin: the ideology of liberal globalization was attacked, and some of the rules that made it work were practically unseated.

At this point, with the aggression of February 24, the actions of Vladimir Putin have undermined the system of liberal globalization and the free market, disrupting the circulation of goods and the globally integrated cycle of production.

The collapse of the United States as a nation state is at this point an ongoing process that can hardly be stopped by political will. But the collapse of this political monster does not in itself open up the prospect of peaceful evolution. On the contrary, the disintegration of the political entity called the United States does not imply the deactivation of the global control platforms that are an offshoot of American power. I'm talking about the military infrastructure that connects men and machines around the world (the Pentagon); I'm talking about the infrastructure that connects every networked point in the world (broadband); I'm talking about the logistical infrastructure that allows one to move people and physical goods; and of course I'm talking the financial infrastructure, which in the last forty years has played a decisive role in the political subjugation of populations. These infrastructures do not depend on the political decision of nation states; on the contrary, nation states have become mere articulations of these global entities, without which social survival would be impossible.

The United States is probably in the process of a political implosion, but global infrastructures will not implode with the dissolution of their formal container, the nation state. On the contrary, they will strengthen their hold on the social body, at all costs, even the destruction of the social body itself. The monster will not die before having caused a global disaster, and I fear that America, understood as a jumble of infrastructural automatisms, will not disappear without a final act of extermination.

This is the geopolitical horizon of the third decade of this century.

Extra-State Infrastructure and Bio-Power

Nations are no longer the site of real power. This is why nationalists raise their voice: they feel that national sovereignty is melting into air and that white domination is fading.

The real source of power resides in those global operating systems that Keller Easterling names "extrastatecraft":

> Today, more than grids of pipes and wires, infrastructure includes pools of microwaves beaming from satellites and populations of atomized electronic devices that we hold in our hands. The shared standards and ideas that control everything also constitute an infrastructure.[5]

Easterling refers to these structures as automated connections that act as enablers of semio-economic exchange in social concatenation. We can describe these infrastructures as

---

5   Keller Easterling (2016) *Extrastatecraft: The Power of Infrastructure Space*, Verso Books, p. 11.

Gestalten (forms that have the power to generate forms). "Like an operating system, the medium of infra-structure space makes certain things possible and other things impossible."[6]

Making possible and making impossible: this is the most fundamental definition of power. This is what Michel Foucault calls "*dispositive*." "Infrastructure space, with its power and currency of software, is an operating system for shaping the city."[7]

In the last half century, the relationship between the anthroposphere and the technosphere has changed to the point of reversal. Since the Paleolithic, man has mediated her relation with nature thanks to the technical concretion of intelligence, and thanks to the making of tools that extend the force of intentional acts. Intentions drive the tool towards a goal. Science materialized under the shape of a technical tool, replacing human fatigue with machines.

In late modern times, a process has developed whereby the technical tool has transformed into a technosphere: this is simultaneously an extroversion of the technical tool, turning it into an integrated environment, and also as introjection of the technological concatenation in the individual mind and in the social organism as a whole.

Media are no longer media, but innervations of a body-swarm, no longer technical exteriorities, but articulations connecting movements and mental projections of the collective turning connective.

The networked concatenation of digital technologies penetrates languages and cognitive activity to the point of conquering the autopoietic ability of the human.

No longer a tool used for intentional, autonomous action,

---

6   *Ibid.*, p. 92.
7   *Ibid.*, p. 13.

technology becomes the automaton, an environment in which the human moves with less and less ability to choose. In the technosphere, the human cannot consume or communicate if not speaking the language of the automaton itself, if not in conformation with the digital net.

Intelligent technologies combine in automated platforms of language and interaction — platforms of enabling — which quickly become indispensable functions of the social organism. These infrastructures submit chaos to the order of the algorithm; however, the automation of the human biosphere is an asymptotic task, and it is impossible to fulfill this project. Notwithstanding this impossibility, the process of automation never stops; it is always expanding and perfecting itself, asymptotically.

The automaton superimposes a bio-totalitarian grid on the life of the world, and now we have begun to distinguish the lines and the articulations of this grid, of this *Ur-Gestalt*. Since 2020, the virus has acted as a chaotic agent on the body and has temporarily disarticulated the automaton. The same can be said of the Ukranian war: it is a chaotic disarticulation of the geopolitical and economic order which prefigures further militarization of the planet, of research, and of production.

Chaos and automation involve, exclude, and follow each other in a continuous spiral. The virus has produced effects of chaos that have caused the automation of the healthcare sphere and the mandatory submission to vaccination regulations. The war is producing effects of chaos that are the prelude to a leap forward in the automation of crime, destruction, and extermination.

The Double Spiral of Chaos and Automation

Two opposite trends are visible: the first is the assembling of automated interconnections asymptotically approaching the establishment of a global cognitive Automaton. Large amounts of data are captured from the daily life of crowds and interfaced with intelligent devices so that new events are reduced to the implementation of a deterministic program. The second trend, however, is the proliferation of chaotic agents triggering ungovernable processes in the fields of geopolitics, economy, and the psychosphere.

It is therefore difficult to predict if the future-scape will be marked by the rigid determinism of digital automatisms or by the chaotic enchainment of multiple processes of disintegration of the social order. The most likely landscape of the future, however, is the interweaving of Chaos and the Automaton, of deterministic chains of interconnected automation and spreading flows of ungovernability and instability.

Order, concocted by political power and technological automation, is now jeopardized by the growing complexity of cultural flows, social conflicts, and unpredictable events: the pandemic, the war; events that change the symbolic attribution of meaning and value.

The biological concrete acts as a factor of indetermination, so after decades of digital and monetary de-materialization of the processes of production, after decades of abstraction of social activity at large, in the wake of the viral outbreak we have experienced a comeback of concreteness.

The physical body has awakened from its long digital oblivion.

Iron, wood, flesh, air, nuclear power plants, and the collective psychology have their own dynamics that do not depend on abstraction. These dynamics have been resurrected by the spreading virus, an invisible agent of chaos.

The virus has been the harbinger of a return of biology into the kingdom of abstraction. But the return of biological matter has unchained waves of chaos in the domain of abstraction, while pushing towards new levels and new modes of abstraction itself. The spiral of Automation and Chaos can be seen as a spiral of indetermination and re-determination at the heart of the social fabric.

The revenge of concreteness has chaotically interrupted the daily business of life and broken supply chains of raw materials and semi-finished products at several points. Those disruptions have continued to accumulate, even if the danger of the virus seems contained by mass vaccination; and what is worse, disruptions have fueled new fronts of instability and conflict.

The Ukrainian War has been part of this explosion of chaotic rear fronts resulting from viral chaos. Biological and psychological concreteness have rendered abstraction chaotic, and at the same time the pandemic has forced everyone to transfer increasing shares of social time into cyberspace, expanding the role of the incorporeal in communication, work, and education.

In terms of social morphogenesis — that is, the creation of new shapes for social systems — the collapse of a system was once considered an opportunity for radical change. Today, the project of revolution seems to be out of the picture, because it is based on the illusion of the potency of will.

In the past, revolution was generally bound to give birth to violent and totalitarian systems, but it was effective. Revolutions did not fulfill their utopian project, but they turned social collapses into radical system changes, opening the way for the shift of political power and the creation of new forms of economic and social lifestyles.

Neoliberalism has been the last effective revolution in human history. It has turned the social turbulence of the 1970s and technological evolution of the 1980s into a sort of market-driven automated game of overall competition; it has therefore created a totalitarian system, abolished the modern bourgeois democracy, and replaced it with the automation of the financial-corporate rationale. But it has also accelerated productivity to the point of saturation, fragmenting labor and making it precarious, a mutation of the social body. In particular, it has destroyed democracy and the effectiveness of political action.

Nevertheless disruptions happen more and more often. However, these are disruptions without revolution. The more complex a system grows, the more it is inclined to disruption. At the same time, the more complex a system grows, the less it is susceptible to voluntary control, and therefore to conscious and intentional change.

In the past age of slow info-circulation and of political governability, disruptions were considered triggers of social morphogenesis. During a disruption, power was weakened and social forces were mobilized, giving way to revolution. In conditions of low complexity (situations where the speed of the information flowing in the social circuit was slow enough for the situation to be consciously governed by human will) political reason was able to change the social organization in such a way that a new pattern could emerge. But under the present conditions, disruptions are unable to give way to revolution, and often they give way to consolidation. Morphostasis, rather than morphogenesis, now follows disruption. The double spiral of chaos and automation has been the general form of the techno-economic domain of semio-capital.

Desertion

Exodus without a Promised Land

Exodus and Leviathan are the two mythological images that powerfully traverse the tradition of our political thought.

Lucio Castellano, *Il potere degli altri*[1]

At the beginning of the 1980s, Michael Walzer's book *Exodus and Revolution* raised a certain interest in circles of the revolutionary left that were undergoing defeat after defeat and being dismantled by the neoliberal offensive.

Exodus and Revolution was intended to retrace the mythological origin of the style of thought and action that characterizes the entire history of the West, particularly political revolutionary thought, and the idea that politics is an action intended to reach some kind of promised land (of justice, freedom, and so on). The origin of this conception of politics can be found, according to Walzer, in an episode from the Bible: the Exodus, in which the Jewish people, led by Moses and with the help of God, flee Egypt and traverse the Red Sea to the Promised Land of Israel.

According to Walzer, the force of this Exodus myth lies in the consciousness that there is a larger world out there, that there are another places out there. Without this consciousness,

---

1   Lucio Castellano (1981) *Il potere degli altri*, Firenze, p. 9.

oppression would be perceived as inevitable, becoming a question of destiny. Without the Promised Land, the Jews' act of rebellion against the Pharaoh would have been meaningless, and no positive solution could have been imagined. In the anthropological area of the great monotheistic religions have been imagined the condition of imaginability of revolution, which comprises not only spontaneous rebellion against the oppressor, but also the institution of an order based on justice. This is the promise that God made to the Jewish people.

We are now on the brink of an exodus that is not heading to any promised land.

The Actuality of Günther Anders

In the 1960s, with the nuclear bomb looming large in the world's imagination, Günther Anders started to reflect on the political and psychological effects of this techno-military innovation.

A German and a Jew, and a philosopher of Heideggerian formation, Anders migrated to America during the Holocaust. He wrote that the Third Reich was only the dress rehearsal for the show that our grandchildren would witness, when Nazism would be everywhere. He was treated with a certain detachment by academics of his time. He was a pessimist, they said, intent on extolling the glories of liberal democracy. Today, Anders' grandchildren are witnessing the triumph of the New Third Reich, the two-headed monster of white supremacy that cannot accept its decline. Now it is clear: the cult of the nation, the cult of race, has returned to rule the stage everywhere, and what is raging in Ukraine is a war of Hitler against Hitler, a war of extermination within the West.

This is not the first time that a white power (i.e., the United States of America) has launched an extermination campaign against a defenseless population. Thanks to the sanctions leveled against Iraq in the first Gulf War, infant mortality rose from 56 per 1,000 in 1990 to 131 per 1,000 in 1999.[2] In 1996, *Sixty Minutes* interviewed the US ambassador to the UN, Madeleine Albright: "Apparently five hundred thousand Iraqi children have died from the embargo. That's more than Hiroshima. Is that a fair price to pay?" The reply was worthy of the Putin we now see in action: "It was a really tough call, but yes, we think it was a fair price to pay."[3]

But those dead were Iraqis — they did not weigh much on the Western conscience. The deaths in Mariupol particularly impress us because the massacre is taking place within the white world, within the West; Russia is the West, in the sense that it is part of the flesh-eating race.

What the "West" is exactly is unclear. In geographical terms, Russia is not part of it. In political terms, the West is the "free world" that opposes autocracy. And of course, geopolitics matters, and politics matters. But what matters more is a cultural tradition of Christian, white imperialism. From this point of view, Russia is the West. The West is the land of decline, the land of the now declining future. Russian futurism and Western futurism have different roots but the same meaning: expansion. And they have the same destiny: the decline that we are not even capable of thinking about because the cult of expansion blinds us and prevents us from realizing that it's over and the West is dying out.

---

2 Tim Dyson and Valeria Cetorelli, "Changing Views on Child Mortality and Economic Sanctions in Iraq: A History of Lies, Damned Lies and Statistics," *BMJ Global Health*. 2017; 2(2): e000311. Published online 2017 Jul 24. doi: 10.1136/bmjgh-2017-000311.

3 Rahul Mahajan, "We Think the Price Is Worth It," *Fair*, 1 November 2001. Available online at: https://fair.org/extra/we-think-the-price-is-worth-it/

The West is Russia, America, Europe; a world of old men who exorcise dementia with cognitive prostheses and artificial intelligence; of old men who exorcise impotence with proclamations of mutual extermination.

This is an internal war within a carnivorous race that does not resign itself to disappearing, and which like Samson wants to take the entire planet with it to hell. We are in the last act of white (Russian, European, and American) civilization: the destruction of civilization.

In a Village at the Border

In March 2022, I read that in a village on the Polish border, a dozen deserters were arriving every night. Tens of thousands of women and children were fleeing every day, but the men had to stay and fight. Some — very few, in truth — did not want to be trapped in a nationalist war, perhaps because this idea of nationhood did not convince them any more than it would have convinced me.

But at the same time, news came that Russian soldiers quartered around Kyiv were abandoning their tanks and heading into the woods to disappear to who knows where. And thousands of young Russians were fleeing to Scandinavia and elsewhere. They did not want to be conscripted by Putin to go and kill their Ukrainian peers; they did not want to live in a country where free speech is persecuted. They took few things with them and left, never to return. When Putin called for national mobilization, five hundred young people fled Russia and became nomadic deserters.

Why do they desert? Perhaps they are in love and do not want to perish. Perhaps they are frightened by the horror and do not want to kill. In any case, to them goes my solidarity, my friendship. Only to them. To *all* those who desert goes my friendship: to those who desert the homeland and war; to those who desert wage labor; to those who desert procreation; to those who desert political participation; to those who have realized that cancer has now devoured the organism and are looking for areas of survival and sharing on the fringes of a rapidly disintegrating world. For those others who are proud of their bloody nations, both Russians and Ukrainians, both Americans and Italians, I feel only desperate compassion.

The deserters are my brothers. They are the only ones who have the courage to flee in the face of the idiocy of peoples and nations. But the deserters are also the symbol of a trend that I see emerging in world history at the twilight of civilization.

Civilization is undergoing accelerated disintegration. You cannot fail to see this.

Mankind is barbarizing at a rapid rate.

The defection that I see emerging in the consciousness of the precarious generation, those threatened with extinction by the climate apocalypse, is defection from the history of mankind.

I am not enunciating a program. I have no intention of inciting desertion. I am only describing a process that can be glimpsed in the behavior of the generation born at the beginning of the millennium: a generation that barely knows the closeness of bodies; a generation that never experienced social solidarity because, from the cradle, it was educated only to look at mobile phone screens and to regard others as competitors for bread.

This generation, which bitterly self-describes itself as the last, might finally find common ground in refusing responsibility for the consequences of their ancestor's ignorance and selfishness.

Branching Off

I see five desertions coalescing in the behavior and language, in the lifestyles and thoughts, of the generation that realizes they have been summoned to live on a planet where it is increasingly difficult to even survive.

Resignation is the first step to desertion, as desertion requires branching off. But resignation to what? Resignation to the fact that the values flaunted by modern culture — economic growth, national identity, representative democracy — no longer mean anything. These values are blurred, dissolved, so better to give up pursuing them if one does not want to waste time on ghosts.

Economic competition — the race to produce and consume more and more goods that are harmful or of no use to us — and competition for increasingly precarious and disputed employment has obsessed the penultimate generation. The "last" one no longer wants to compete. It is too exhausted to compete; it is too depressed to compete; it is too ironic to compete. Exhaustion, depression, and irony are marks of a cultural evolution that only later will develop new energy, new happiness, and new assertiveness.

The Great Resignation of workers began to interest economists when, at the end of the Covid-19 pandemic, four and a half million American workers decided not to return to work. In English it is called "resignation." In Italian it is translated as "self-layoff," "abandonment of employment," and also "refusal of work." The signs of this frustration with labor can be traced everywhere, including in China, where journalists have invented a new word that means something like "those who don't want to get out of bed."

Defection from work is not a novelty in the history of class struggle, of course. In the 1970s, young metal workers were struggling against increased productivity and demanded the reduction of work hours. Now it is different: resignation is no longer a conscious refusal, and it is not linked to a political agenda for change. Resignation involves the sudden realization that salaried work is the most stupid way to spend your time, and that our pay only keeps us going from one work day to the next. Those resigning understand that the outcome of our activity is essentially the destruction of the environment and the ruination of our lives.

During the pandemic, governments invested huge amounts of money with the intention of pushing people to consume and save the economy, contributing to the inflation we are currently seeing. Nevertheless, misery is now spreading, and the smart way to avoid misery is by reducing the need for anything that cannot be produced by social autonomy. Self-reliance; independence from the market: it's not easy, but many are trying, and soon everybody will be forced to try if they don't want to starve.

Consumption is not going back to pre-Covid levels: you can bring a horse to water.

The consumer is tired of being a consumer.

Consumerist desire is on a downward trend: psycho-deflation.

It seems to me that the "last generation" could be reducing its consumption partly for ideological reasons (I do not want to contribute to destroying the planet on which I have to live), but above all it is out of a kind of disgust, an aesthetic rejection of consumerist ugliness and the displeasure that plastic arouses in a sensitive person.

Shopping, as a substitute for an interesting emotional life, has marked the miserable lives of a hundred million zombies who had money to spend and found goods to buy. But now the money is gone and so are the goods, thanks to the Great Supply Chain Disruption (God bless it).

From now on, consumerism will be a sign of a cultural and aesthetic backwardness, a sign of the boorishness of the soul.

Subsequently, there has been a third desertion: the alienation of young people from political participation. The levels of electoral absenteeism recorded in the French elections of spring 2022 were unprecedented.[4] The same was true of the Italian local elections of June 2022.[5] Both are countries with a strong tradition of political participation.

I would say that faith in representative democracy is over because everyone now realizes that democratic governments, like authoritarian ones, can do nothing against environmental catastrophe. They cannot do the only reasonable thing: renounce the unquestionable principle of economic growth. They can do nothing against financial dominance. They can do nothing against psychic suffering. They can do nothing at all. So why do they waste our time with their feigned disputes, insults, and emptiness?

In addition, of course, there is the desertion of war as it ravages ever larger areas of the world. In the early days of the Ukrainian War, deserters amounted to a few dozen a day, but these were but a vanguard; perhaps they have become more numerous in the meantime. They will certainly grow in number as time goes on.

---

4   Lou Roméo, "Voter turnout issue looms over French legislative elections after record first-round abstention," *France24*, 15 June 2022. Available online at: https://www.france24.com/en/france/20220615-voter-turnout-issue-looms-over-french-legislative-elections-after-record-first-round-ab-stention

5   Paul Kirby, "Giorgia Meloni: Italy's far-right wins election and vows to govern for all," *BBC News*, 26 September 2022. Available online at: https://www.bbc.com/news/world-europe-63029909

Finally, there is the most important desertion of all: desertion of procreation. The birth-rate incentives offered by northern states (from China, to Italy, to almost all other countries that have achieved a certain level of welfare) are having no effect. How to explain this trend? My explanation is quite simple: consciously and unconsciously women are deciding not to generate the victims of climate hell, the victims of coming nuclear war.

It must be said that the birth strike of a majority of women worldwide is compounded by a collapse in male fertility. Stacey Colino and Shanna Swan write in their book *Count Down* that "sperm counts have plummeted by 50 percent in the last forty years" (you read that right: *50 percent*).[6] According to Colino and Swan, the main cause of this infertility is the spread of microplastics in the food chain. It seems that microplastics are involved in hormonal transmission or something, and their spread in the environment is the main (but not the only) cause of the decrease in fertility (as if to say: every cloud has a silver lining).

Five desertions. This, in my opinion, is going to be an unstoppable trend, only partly conscious (or even totally unconscious), towards non-involvement: that is, towards autonomy.

But some may ask: How will we survive in desertion? To answer, I return to the magic word: "re-signation," which in English can mean (if we like — after all, words mean what we decide they do) "re-signification," an act of rewriting signs and reassigning signifiers.

---

6   Stacey Colino and Shanna H. Swan (2021) *Count Down: Our Modern World Is Threatening Sperm Counts, Altering Male and Female Reproductive Development, and Imperiling the Future of the Human Race*, Scribner, p. 12.

In the search for a new sense of existing, action no longer coincides with the order of work, sustaining oneself no longer coincides with consumption, love has nothing to do with starting a family and bringing into the world innocents to whom we cannot even guarantee the minimum wage of survival, and finally, politics no longer has anything to do with government, with representation and representativeness. And obviously desert war, desert national rhetorics.

Passivism and Defection from Work

As political will has proven impotent in the field of both governance and understanding, psychoanalysis must open itself to the comprehension of phenomena that do not belong only to the individual sphere.

The pathology that psychiatrists name "depressive psychosis" cannot be treated exclusively at the individual level. What kind of therapeutic technique can be of help at this juncture?

Let's think about what Paul Watzlawick calls "paradoxical therapies," which can be based on the prescription of the symptom.

As the symptom is a depressive syndrome based on protracted impotence, try to conceive of depressive impotence as a systemic adaptation that will evolve through extended group therapy. Listen to the meaning of your depression, and recognize the truth that your depression brings with it in a collective framework. The community of the hopeless may be a good starting point for going beyond the present suffering and transforming it into conscious disinvestment.

The depressive mind-set can be restructured through an intentional *mise en scene* of the symptom. Passivity is a means of preparing to abandon a problematic field, the scene of a trauma.

The prolonged perception of powerlessness has brought social subjectivity to a crossroads: we must choose between aggressive identity extroversion or passivity.

For the predominant culture, passivity appears as the problem. Let's try to see it as the solution.

I think that a mighty passivist movement is burrowing beneath the visible surface of post-pandemic social life. This may be the way out of the hyper-productive, hyper-communicative syndrome that has led us to collapse.

By withdrawing social energy, passivism can bring to a halt the production-consumption cycle that forces us to give up life.

What is happening in the labor movement can be described from this point of view, and the behavior of some workers seems to signal a sort of spreading, passive refusal of capitalist rule. Paul Krugman has been writing about this phenomenon in the last year or so: "What seems to be happening instead is that the pandemic led many U.S. workers to rethink their lives and ask whether it was worth staying in the lousy jobs too many of them had."[7]

But why are we experiencing what many are calling "the Great Resignation," with so many workers either quitting or demanding higher pay and better working conditions? Until recently, conservatives blamed expanded unemployment benefits, claiming that these benefits were reducing the incentive to work.

---

7   Paul Krugman, "The Revolt of the American Worker, " *New York Times*, 14 October 2021. Available online at: https://www.nytimes.com/2021/10/14/opinion/workers-quitting-wages.html

It is quite possible that the pandemic, by upending many Americans' lives, also caused some of them to reconsider their life choices. Not everyone can afford to quit a hated job, but a significant number of workers seem ready to accept the risk of trying something different — retiring earlier, despite the monetary cost, looking for a less unpleasant job in a different industry, and so on.

Companies have difficulty finding labor not because unemployment has disappeared, but because an increasing number of humans have decided that working is a renunciation of life, a perpetual humiliation. Given the stagnation of wages and the precariousness of existence, refusing work is the only rational choice.

Simultaneously, a parallel event is shaking the normalcy of social production: disruptions in the production cycle and the global supply chain proliferate. The Great Supply Chain Disruption and the Great Resignation are two sides of a single phenomenon: the dissolution of the physical and psychological conditions for the extraction of work and for the organization of the global cycle. The energy that drives capital refuses to be mobilized, and this is provoking a crack in the infrastructure of the daily business of life.

Since the beginning of the pandemic, the concept of psycho-deflation has allowed me to understand this fall in energy, this crumbling of the social order, and this spreading of chaos. Far from seeing psycho-deflation as a disease, I propose to see it as a lever with which to destroy capitalist automation so that we can finally emerge from the infected corpse of capitalism.

Resignation is a process of restructuring the imaginary field, and can disclose perspectives that otherwise remain hidden by inherited cultural expectations. Furthermore, resignation makes possible a relaxation of the tension that generates panic, and allows one to finally prepare oneself for a future without any more pathogenic hope.

The signs of resignation are multiplying: a spring 2021 survey of an international sample of adults revealed that 39 percent of respondents did not want to have children.[8]

A kind of resignation to extinction is emerging, almost a strategy of self-extinction that paradoxically may turn out to be the only way out of extinction. This is a providential mass repudiation of procreation, work, consumption, and participation. Humans are deciding to abandon the game.

Is this a problem? In my opinion, it is the solution.

Resigning ourselves to the end of growth is the only way to reduce energy consumption. Detoxing from the anxiety of consumption and educating each other about frugality is the only way to escape the stress and system of blackmail that forces us to accept slave labor.

Deserting procreation is the only way to reduce the demographic pressure that produces overcrowding, violence, war.

The strategy of desertion is articulated in the following principles:

One: Do not participate in the democratic fiction that leads one to believe that by appointing someone else as one's representative, the irreversible can become reversible.

Two: Do not work. Work is increasingly underpaid, increasingly less guaranteed, increasingly exploited, and

---

8   Elizabeth Marks et al., "Young People's Voices on Climate Anxiety, Government Betrayal and Moral Injury: A Global Phenomenon," *The Lancet*, 2021; 5: e863–73, DOI:10.2139/ssrn.3918955

increasingly useless for the production of the necessary. Let us devote our energies to care, to the transmission of knowledge, to research, to self-sufficiency. Let us break all relations with the economy.

Three: No longer consume anything that is not produced by self-producing communities. Boycott the circulation of goods.

Four: Do not procreate. Procreation is a selfish and irresponsible act when the chances of a happy life are reduced to almost zero. It is a dangerous act because the habitable areas of the planet are shrinking and the population is growing.

Five: Do not participate in any war, do not defend any borders. Do not attack, but do not defend against aggression either. Simply abandon, abandon, abandon.

In this gesture of retraction there is a principle of autonomy: emancipation from the *Squid Game*. Resignation from work is not merely a sign of resignation, but an act of self-affirmation by thinking subjects abandoning the corpse of capitalism.

This phenomenon is by no means limited to the United States, but has a global character, and since the autumn of 2021, it has begun to spread, to become chronic. Desertion from work may become the most powerful lever we have to bring down neoliberal domination of human life.

Workers quitting work is neither a good thing nor a bad thing *per se*: it is a signal of alienation that can be transformed into active and conscious desertion; that is, it can be turned into autonomy by giving meaning to abandonment, passivity, and resignation.

There is no longer any reason to lend our time to a society

that is clearly no longer able to give us anything, neither health, nor education, nor peace, nor a decent wage.

I believe that this is the theoretical and political task of the time to come: to redefine activity according to a principle of frugal utility and the enjoyment of an existence free from the imperative to function; to redefine our activity in relation to concrete usefulness and pleasurableness — not in relation to abstract economic valor.

Concreteness comes back. In recent years it has returned as an explosion of chaos and of suffering. But the castle of abstraction may be made to crumble.

The Revenge of Concreteness

Steel and Finance

While the tanks proceed along the Ukrainian roads and the bombs fall spreading terror, Western countries respond with an offensive of words, figures, and sanctions that operate in the sphere of finance, the virtual avatar of the economy. The exclusion of Russia from the SWIFT circuit, the blocking of Visa and Mastercard on Russian territory, and a series of financial boycott measures aim to stop the aggression. But the aggression goes on.

The military system, and in particular the production of weapons, has been, and will increasingly be, a decisive pillar of the world economy. But as soon as the weapons have been built, thanks to the money, as soon as the soldiers have been trained to use the weapons, the steel machine goes on giving a damn about finance.

The sanctions against Russia have not worked so well. The European economy has entered into recession, while the Russian economy has been doing better: 2.6 of growth in the year 2023.

Biden and Johnson have drawn the Ukrainian people into a deadly confrontation, and two years after we know that Ukraine is broken, Germany is in the throes of an economic downturn, while the Russian economy has been resilient, and the American economy is going full steam.

Two years after the invasion we are allowed to say that America has won the war against Germany and against the

European Union, while Russia is poised to win the war against Ukraine.

Russian society has been pushed into a war system, and it will take time, perhaps a lot of time, before Putin's military power is destroyed by the effects of the financial boycott. Meanwhile he is carrying out the devastation of Ukrainian society, the fragmentation of the European Union, and the destabilization of the world order.

What attracts my attention here is a fact whose implications go beyond military strategy: materiality, which in recent decades had been weakened and almost erased by the apparent omnipotence of abstraction (particularly financial abstraction), has awakened, and like a zombie rising from a long torpor, it is acting in an irrepressible and chaotic way.

Iron, wood, flesh, air, nuclear power plants, and the collective psyche — all these different material things have their own dynamics, independent of the abstract orders within which they are conceived. Almighty finance seems for the first time powerless in the face of the brute force that unleashes the elements making up the concrete of life.

The psychic depression that can be glimpsed beyond the pandemic horizon, the panic that erupts in crowd movements and in the loneliness of distant individuals, accumulates and results in rituals of aggressive exorcism.

War is a cure (more dangerous than any other) for collective depression.

Psychic concreteness turns the order of the Automaton into Chaos.

The Biological Concrete

The first revelation of this revenge of the concrete came in the spring of 2020, when an infinitely small material concretion, called a virus, spread speedily in the bodies that inhabit the world, producing a paralysis of social life, of consumption and production, chaotically interrupting the supply chains of raw materials, semi-finished products, and finished products at several points.

Those disruptions have continued to accumulate, even if the danger of the virus seems contained by mass vaccination, and what is worse, these disruptions create new fronts of instability and conflict. The Ukrainian War is part of this explosion of chaotic effects resulting from viral chaos.

The biological concrete has chaotized the financial abstract, but at the same time, the pandemic has forced everyone to transfer increasing shares of social time into cyberspace, expanding the extent of the incorporeal.

Simultaneously, the pandemic has brought the people's concrete needs to the surface: the need for medicines, vaccines, and food for a population that feels besieged by an invisible but very concrete agent.

The invisible concrete has thus short-circuited the invisible abstraction of finance. The financial world did not suffer from the pandemic; on the contrary, the stock markets continued an upward trend, favored in particular by the amazing profits of the pharmaceutical and digital cycles, the latter of which manufacture indispensable tools for distancing. Nevertheless, its hold on the concreteness of planetary life is failing. Money does not work to heal malady, it does not work to ease the spreading fear, and at present it seems that money is unable to stop the rage and fire of the war.

For decades, capital has ensured the integrated functioning of global distribution, stimulated largely unnecessary and harmful consumption, and compensated for existential misery with a constant supply of consumer shit. But now this compensation is crumbling. Between 2020 and 2021, the price of shipping from the US to Asian countries multiplied tenfold,[1] and from April 2021, the price of gas and electricity started to soar in all European countries.[2]

The disconnection of global cycles manifests itself in effects of chaos in the global economy. Capitalism has entered a chaotic phase from which it will hardly be able to exit using the levers of finance and monetary stimulus, because this chaos depends on the sphere of the concrete, of bodies that get sick, of minds that go crazy, of physical goods that float on the ocean, of factories blocked by the lack of semifinished products. Financial leverage has begun to run in circles.

Economics Is a Dead Science

The economist Paul Krugman, in his columns for the *New York Times*, insists repeatedly that American workers who complain about the state of the economy are wrong. Wages are rising, growth is booming, and the numbers are going up — what more do you want? He is, however, unable to see a quite simple reality: people are suffering no matter how much money they earn. This inability to understand what is happening in the real (that is, the mental) life of society is the clearest sign of a disconnect between the economy of accumulation and the well-being of society.

Economics is the science of the abstract, or rather it is a

---

1   Roslan Khasawneh and Muyu Xu, "China-U.S. container shipping rates sail past $20,000 to record," *Reuters*, 6 August 2021. Available online at: https://www.reuters.com/business/china-us-container-shipping-rates-sail-past-20000-record-2021-08-05/

2   Jorge Liboreiro and Alberto de Filippis, "Why Europe's energy prices are soaring and could get much worse," *Euronews*, 28 October 2021. Available online from: https://www.euronews.com/my-europe/2021/10/28/why-europe-s-energy-prices-are-soaring-and-could-get-much-worse

technique aimed at submitting concrete life to the logic of the accumulation of abstract value. Therefore it is completely useless to understand well-being and malaise. The only function of the economy is to move more abstract value away from society towards big capital. But now the bottom of the barrel has been scraped. There is nothing left for anyone.

Malaise spreads regardless of the amount of money that is given to us in exchange for our dead labor. What we need is not money — money cannot be used buy what no longer exists: affection, pleasure, time, hope, happiness, and also food, medicine, and water. Of course, this is completely incomprehensible to poor Krugman, even if he is the best economist in the world. Once upon a time, when candidates won elections thanks to good economic performance, we used to say, "it's the economy, stupid." Now we should rather say, "it's psychology stupid," because candidates are winning elections by exploiting the psychopathology of the majority.

The world order seems more and more shaky, we must be aware of this.

The effect of the inter-Nazi war that is taking place in Ukraine will be the collapse of the European economy, the collapse of the financial system, and the spread of inter-ethnic conflicts throughout Europe. Depressive psychosis will mix with rash panic.

The economy is dead because money won't help much unless you have enough of it to hire Elon Musk's shuttle and fly away.

The Double Defeat of Thought

The man stands between life and death
The man thinks
The horse thinks
The sheep thinks
The cow thinks
The dog thinks
The fish doesn't think
The fish is mute, expressionless
The fish doesn't think because the fish knows everything
Goran Bregović and Iggy Pop, This Is a Film

Thinking

A concept is a set of inseparable variations that is produced or constructed on a plane of immanence insofar as the latter crosscuts the chaotic variability and gives it consistency (reality). A concept is therefore a chaoid state par excellence; it refers back to a chaos rendered consistent, become Thought, mental chaosmos.
Gilles Deleuze and Félix Guattari, What Is Philosophy?[1]

Thinking is the function of transformation of conceptual constructs which allow us to conceive a world and to move inside that world.

---

1   Deleuze and Guattari, *What Is Philosophy?*, p. 208.

Thought traverses the space of consciousness, decomposing and recomposing it, and leaning out, overlooks the chaos that surrounds consciousness, overlooks the shadows that invade the margins of the space enlightened by concepts.

Deleuze and Guattari write in the last pages of *What is Philosophy?* that concepts and sensations share the same shadow, which extends across them and never ceases to accompany them.

There is a shadow all around the light of concepts, precepts, and affects. This shadow is chaos, the pre-semiotic and pre-sensitive magma. Consciousness is the pilot that guides us through this crossing: experience.

Consciousness is the ensemble of ritournelles that we are dancing while moving in the chaotic shadow that surrounds our sentient organism.

It sometimes happens that constructs fixate, that ritournelles stiffen congeal such that consciousness repeats and repeats the same ritournelle out of sync. Because sometimes the ritournelles are unable to concatenate with the music of chaos. Ritournelles fixate as an obsession.

Neuroscientists are making the hypothesis that our cognitive behavior is shaped by a sort of default mode network, a web of ritournelles that we have inherited or processed. They help us to navigate, but sometime we should get rid of them, such as when they stiffen and become obsessive.

At this point, the activity of thinking beings, which creates new concatenations, new ritournelles that give consciousness the capacity to jump, to step into another dimension, another environment, into a new (provisional) harmony beyond chaos, at the border of chaos.

Thought is the function of the transformation of consciousness, which in turn is the function of self-reflection of the subject that perceives and conceptualizes the world. Consciousness leads the subject, as a sentient cartography of the environment, as a way of orienting itself in the forest of perceptual projections and conceptual emanations. This conscious roaming around sometimes turns problematic, as the environment changes and unpredictable situations arise. Consciousness must adapt, change, jump, conjoin with new flows, and disconnect from the old. Thinking gives you the capacity to create new links, new pathways in the fires of existence.

What about thinking in these times?

Belonging

In his 1987 book *La defaite de la pensée* (*The Defeat of Thought*), Alain Finkielkraut speaks of the defeat of thought. For Finkielkraut, culture, a particular form of the identity of a people, affirms itself to the detriment of thought, whose universalist character is criticized in the name of cultural relativity and abandoned in the name of identity belonging: white, black, Islamic, gay, Lombard, Hindu, Serb, Croat, Basques, and so on in a endless Borgesian list of imaginary absoluteness.

Culture, explains Finkielkraut, is the legacy of mythological, ethical, and aesthetic values that we inherit from history. It is an inheritance that we receive through belonging and which confirms this belonging, this being of ours that opposes all becoming, that fears becoming and rejects it. Therefore, thought is the irruption of becoming-other into cultural continuity.

Culture claims its authenticity, which is nothing but an illusion. But the illusion is projected onto the world as a desire for reduction, as an identity conflict.

This dialectics of thought and culture drive the dynamics of civilization, of democracy, of respect for the other, and of ethical life. In late modernity, the crisis of Enlightenment and of the ethical principle of universality is a direct consequence of the assertive comeback of *Kultur* as identity: as the particularity that reclaims its own history, its own tradition. It is being resisting becoming.

In the following years, Finkielkraut's intuition proved dramatically prophetic. The Union of Soviet Socialist Republics, an attempt to found a political entity on ideological principles rather than on the identity of a people, collapsed under the pressure of Western countries and as a result of the centrifugal forces of the religious and national ethnic identities within it (Ukrainians, Lithuanians, Latvians, Armenians, Azerbaijani, Tatars, Kalmyks, and so on). As we know, the end of the Soviet Union was not the beginning of a period of prosperity and democracy, and national identity regained the upper hand in the various territories that began to tear themselves apart. This tragedy is still unfolding, as testified to by the evolution of the Armenian-Azerbaijani conflict, and by the war between Russians and Ukrainians that began on 24 February 2022.

Furthermore, in the 1990s, pressure from international finance, the Vatican, and the Deutsche Bundesbank caused the collapse of another internationalist entity, Yugoslavia. The Yugoslav War marked the return of an ethnic and nationalist ferocity we had believed to be dead and buried after the end of Nazism.

In 1996, when the Yugoslav War had already shown the ferocity of the emerging post-ideological world, Finkielkraut published *L'humanité perdue* (*Lost Humanity*), in which he tackled the same problem as in the previous book, but from a different perspective: the exhaustion of modern humanism after the tragic dissolution of the universal ideologies of the twentieth century. "After the pathology of History, a new not less obnoxious pathology is threatening to run amok throughout the world: Geography."[2]

In the last three decades, the defeat of thought has taken the shape of the cult of belonging, which took center-stage on the global scene in 2016 when the British decided to quit Europe for the sake of their national superiority and an aggressive, ignorant tycoon won the American presidential election in the name of the superiority of the white race.

The rule of cultural belonging (in the sense of Kultur, as opposed to *Bildung*) makes thought ineffectual.

The defeat of universalist thought comes with the spread of chaos, the new king of the world. Chaos is the visible face of Nothing. The nothing of identity and the deception of belonging have overwhelmed thought, subjugating thinking to mythologies that want to be revealed truths, and paving the way to violence. In the name of this nothing that is identity, peoples become nations through war, and only war certifies the incontrovertible truth of nothing.

Simultaneously, another defeat of thought is underway on another front: cognitive automation.

Automation

So far I have dealt with the historical side of thought's defeat: cultural identity, which forbids thinking for the sake of belonging. There is, however, another side to this defeat: the technological. This is the automation of cognitive

---

2   Alain Finkielkraut (1996) *L'humanité perdue*, Seuil, p. 140. "*Après la maladie de l'Histoire, une autre fureur, plus comique mais non moins nocive, affecte les hommes et menace de rendre le monde amok: la maladie de la géographie.*"

activity, a replacement of thinking processes and of critical discrimination with programs inscribed in the linguistic machine and in social governance.

This trend was first perceived in the 1960s in the context of critical thinking of idealist derivation. "Technological reasoning," writes Marcuse in *One Dimensional Man*, "tends to identify things and their function."[3] "The subject of thought becomes the pure and universal form of subjectivity, from which all particulars are removed.[4]

In the 1950 and '60s, while technical evolution created the first cybernetic machines and Hubert Dreyfus wondered about the distinction between the human brain and electronic computers, Marcuse wrote of the reduction of knowledge to the operative function — digital coding.

Due to information technology and the consequent digitization of information, the conscious organism has come into contact with semiotic machines capable of transferring information, but above all of identifying the operational meaning of a sign. These machines interfere with the flow of communication, simulating the functioning of the language agent to the point of automatically reproducing cognitive behavior. It is a process of assimilation of automaton and organism, in one sense or another.

The execution of the automaton is more and more a simulation of the intentional human act, and symmetrically, the human mind is induced to act more and more as if it were an automaton. The automation of cognitive processes coincides with the abolition of thinking.

As the machine imitates cognition more and more, and

---

3   Herbert Marcuse, *One-Dimensional Man*, Routledge, p. 90.

4   *Ibid.*, pp. 139–40.

simulates human behaviors, cognition and behavior imitate the machine more and more in order to interact with it.

Not only does the machine pervade the social environment, but society itself is assimilated to an automatic model of technologically driven acts.

Will the evolution of cognitive automation lead to the creation of an artificial intelligent organism? Can the simulation of cognitive activity lead to an automated brain?

Neuro-Aesthetics of the Unimaginable

What can we say about the evolution of subjectivity? Has the prolonged suspension of social exchange deactivated the imagination and the collective ability to rebel, organize, invent?

The impending psychosphere is enigmatic.

Simultaneously, after five centuries of the systematic exploitation of nature, nature seems to be taking revenge. After decades of unbridled exploitation of the social brain, the social mind seems to be on the verge of a collapse: nationalism, racism, and paranoid fascism are spreading like furious forest fires, while the cognitive automaton replaces the organic brain in the shaping of social action. The long duel between social autonomy and domination seems to be approaching checkmate.

But wait a moment. As we know, in the sphere of human experience there are two types of games: finite games and infinite games. A finite game is played to win; an infinite game is played to continue the game.

Finite games are those where you absolutely have to follow the rules, because if you don't, then you are simply not playing the game. Think of chess: if you want to play chess, you cannot move the rook as if it were a bishop, or vice versa, and when the king is in a certain position, you can declare that the game is over.

Even infinite games have rules, but the players know well that during the game the rules can be transgressed, exceeded, changed. Think of love; think of war. In those games, the rules exist, but players know they will be betrayed, avoided, reinvented, because that is the only way to continue the game: by evolving.

When we talk about cultural evolution, we are not talking about a finite game that can be won by a player and closed with a checkmate, following the rules. The rules exist, as we know: the economic rule, the political rule, the proprietary rule; mental rules, aesthetic rules. But human history is an infinite game. As long as players are alive, they can break the rules and even change the playing field.

Therefore, we'll not stop rejecting rules, protesting the established order, and escaping cultural conformism. Above all, we must look for a way to broaden the field of the game itself. Imagination is the faculty that allows us to extend what we see of the playing field.

Even if depression is inevitable, even if global civil war is inevitable, even if environmental devastation is inevitable, even if the extinction of mankind is inevitable, we should not forget the phrase of that witty guy John Maynard Keynes, who said, "In general the inevitable does not happen because the unpredictable prevails."

What is the unpredictable in our present situation, which appears marked by the prospect of inevitable catastrophe? Of course, we cannot know, since it is precisely the unpredictable.

Maybe a scientific invention? Maybe a world insurrection? We cannot predict the unpredictable, and we cannot imagine the unimaginable, because imagination is the elaboration of acquired mental experiences towards their recombination into original configurations.

We cannot predict how the traumatic experience of social and physical distancing will evolve in the long run. We cannot predict how the war will change the geopolitical map. We cannot predict how the climatic apocalypse will change daily life in the near future.

The possible is unimaginable, or unthinkable, from the present point of view.

But the present point of view is going to evolve along the lines of the ongoing catastrophe. In fact, the Greek origin of the word "catastrophe" — "*kata-strophein*" — means "moving beyond."

Thought is activity that goes together with catastrophe: the activity of making sense of the unseen landscapes that the catastrophe is deploying before our eyes.

Like aliens just landed on an unknown planet, we are walking a new terrain whose territories decreasingly correspond to the available maps. We need new conceptual tools and new cognitive maps.

When Wittgenstein wrote that we should not speak of what cannot be said, he was referring to the limit of the thinkable, but he was also implying that there are two sides of the wall that is limiting our thought. What is beyond the wall is ineffable, but now it's time to have a look beyond the wall of the already thought. Thinking is about the unthought that lies beyond that wall.

N. Katherine Hayles, in *Unthought: The Power of the Cognitive Nonconscious*, speaks of the relationship between the "sphere of Consciousness" (including the unconscious) and the "sphere of Cognition," which involves the sphere of technology and biological matter. There is a tension between unthought and consciousness: thought is the creation of concepts that confer consistency and dependability on the unknown on the other side of the wall. In order to see beyond the wall, we must perform acts of psychomancy, if I may say so.

Psychomancy doesn't exist, as far as I know, and if it does, it's a weird thing. For me, it means the act of deciphering the imminent intersection between countless mental projections. In order to perform psychomantic acts, it is necessary to imagine the unimaginable, and for this purpose we have some techniques: poetry, insurrection, psychedelia.

We all are going through an experience of multiple traumas. But how can these traumas be processed? How can we happily evolve these multiple traumas? How can we tune in to the catastrophic landscape?

Ethical norms are not helping here, and neither is political will.

The Neuro-Aesthetic Passage

The pandemic revealed the evanescence of the power of the will.

Announcers of modernity Niccolò Machiavelli and Francis Bacon emphasized the relationship between will and power: the first said that the will of the prince can subdue *Fortuna*, the unpredictable variability of events. The second said that knowledge is a multiplier of the power of the will.

But the will possesses power only as long as the anthropocentric principle enunciated by Protagoras is valid: "Man is the measure of all things." Since man is the measure of all things, to a certain extent his will can decide the course of events. But the power of the will fades when relevant world events escape measurement. The proliferation of the virus and the toxic contamination of the physical and mental environment go beyond the range of decision and the power of the will.

That's why I don't expect anything from politics. The bombast of politicians sounds ridiculous. As a bold captain tries in vain to avoid shipwreck when the storm is too big for his sails, so the political leaders of our time show their helplessness when dealing with the viral invasion, with the clouds of radioactivity, and with the flames of climate change, not to mention the collapse of the mental sphere.

The accelerating speed of the infosphere makes governing impossible, and the social world oscillates between chaos and automation. Nervous info-stimulation has become too fast and invasive, so acts of decision-making are progressively subsumed by the language machine: life is captured and subjected to automation. This is why the power of the will dissipates, and humans feel powerless, almost overwhelmed.

I think we should scale back the importance we have bestowed on the cognitive faculty called "will." In order to be able to enter into a relationship with the indeterministic universe of proliferation, we should rather rely on sensitivity.

Sniffing, inhaling, auscultating, looking sideways, glimpsing, squinting, blinking, gazing, lightly touching, caressing. Aesthetics is taking the place of ethics in this passage, because aesthetic sensibility helps us to act like critters who try to map an alien planet in order to inhabit it. Aesthetic attunement is slowly taking the place of political determination. This is where the concept of "neuro-aesthetics" derives all its importance from.

The virus has induced a mutation of the social organism and of the collective unconscious, leading to phobic sensitization to the body of the other: ambiguous depression, abandonment of the field of contention, the withdrawal of desire, disinvestment. In a word, desertion.

Trauma acts to destructure established cognitive links in the dynamic dimension that lies between neurology and (un)consciousness. As an effect of trauma, we are led to discover new possibilities previously hidden by the network of automatic reactions in our brain (also known as the default mode network).

A neuro-aesthetic metamorphosis is underway: this is the search for a *chaosmose*, a relaxed and comfortable interweaving of mental rhythm and the rhythm of chaos. Aesthetics is the field of syntonization.

Ambiguous Praise of Beauty

"Beauty is a fateful gift of the essence of truth," writes Martin Heidegger.[1] I think the contrary: Beauty is a destiny (not the only one) of the absence of truth.

If truth existed, we would have no need for beauty; we would gaze at the true, the eternal, the immovable, and we would be forever absorbed in it. But there is no truth to reveal. The apocalypse reveals nothing if not just this: the absence of a secret to be revealed. The enigmatic apocalypse does not disclose the truth, but it stuns. Then our cognitive habits are interrupted and confused, and we are stunned by the infinite excess of bodies and the limitations of our time, by the impossibility of touching all the bodies we desire, of living all the lives we can imagine.

Beauty is this cruelty of excess pleasure that we cannot enjoy. Beauty is this passion of the excess: not knowing that

---

1   Martin Heidegger (1968) *What is Called Thinking?* HarperPerennial, p. 19.

we cannot know because there is nothing to know, only things to imagine, to think, to create by thinking.

"Exuberance is beauty," says Blake, who also writes: "The road of excess leads to the palace of wisdom."[2] Exuberance means an excess of energy, but also an excess of meaning.

There are caresses, there are substances, there are words capable of initiating an uncertain interpretation of excess: the indecipherable image, the enigmatic word, the poignant desire.

I have always asked myself: What is beauty? But I am yet to find an answer. Having obtained a degree in aesthetics, beauty would be my topic. I am a professional in this field, so to speak. Yet, of one thing I am certain: the more I investigated the subject, the more I questioned myself about it, the more I strayed from the answer.

"A thing of beauty is a joy forever," wrote Keats.[3] I have tried in many ways to understand the meaning of these words, but I have not succeeded. What does beauty have to do with joy? And why should the joy caused by beauty last forever, as the insipid Englishman says?

The infinite fountain of immortal drink that gushes in us at the edge of the sky sounds to my ears like a lie, because if there is anything I think I can say about beauty, it is precisely this: that beauty fades, and in the short time of its appearance gives us nothing.

Dostoevsky wrote that only "beauty will save the world."[4] But his idea of beauty is hysterical, and his heaven is perfect suffering. Russian beauty is the exaltation that comes from pain, because pain brings us closer to God. Forget it. There

---

2   William Blake (1793) "Proverbs of Hell."
3   John Keats (1818) "Endymion."
4   Fyodor Dostoevsky (2004) *The Idiot*, Penguin Classics.

is no God that beauty can bring us close to. We grope, and beauty urges us to grope methodically.

Adorno says that beauty disappears. But even this seems contentious to me.

In our age, beauty is rampant, or at least aesthetic stimulation is rampant. The twentieth century produced a general aestheticization of the world, until the digital introduced an idea of beauty as smoothness and perfection. But the conscious and sensitive organism that connects and enters the world of digital syntactic perfection continues to suffer; indeed it suffers from new pains. And we need poetic inaccuracy if we want to start living happily again.

Paolo Sorrentino's 2013 film *La grande bellezza* (*The Great Beauty*) makes me think that beauty is inseparable from sadness, bitterness, failure, and corruption. In the film, beauty is old. Its protagonist, Jep Gambardella, is asked at the beginning of the film, "What do you really like?" His friends reply, "*La fessa*," while Jep responds, "The smell of old people's rooms." For this he had a high spirit, and when he grew up he became a writer. The perfect beauty is very ugly, like the 104-year-old saint who appears at the end of the film and climbs the stairs, an interminable ordeal, on her knees.

In *American Beauty*, Sam Mendes grasps the ambiguous meaning of beauty in the words of a young filmmaker, Ricky (Wes Bentley), when he shows his neighbor Jane (Thora Birch) what he considers the most beautiful thing he has ever filmed: a plastic bag that flutters in the wind in front of a brick wall. "When I captured that moment, I realized that there is a whole life behind everything." Ricky feels that "sometimes there is so much beauty in the world that I am unable to tolerate it and my heart folds in on itself." America is the ugliest and most repulsive place that God has ever managed to conceive in the whole universe. But Ricky manages to grasp its beauty. Beauty is the sensual perception of excess that simmers in the midst of the horror of reality.

We call beautiful a sign that leads us towards the interpretation of the enigma.

If what we are looking for is an escape route from unhappiness beyond the pandemic threshold, I would say that there is an emerging behavioral trend that could shape evolution in a benign way. This trend is ambiguous: the psycho-deflation we are undergoing can lead to long-term depression, but it can also lead to the proliferation of self-subsisting migrant communities, and a conscious disengagement from the fate of the declining planet and the feelings of the incapable majority in tune with irreversible decline. We should create high-tech and low-tech communities that are interconnected but also prepared to remain in complete isolation for long periods.

The possible outcomes of the long oscillation that is accompanying the processing of pandemic trauma are unpredictable. Frugality could replace acquisitive anxiety. The new generation does not reject consumerism only for ideological reasons, but also out of a creeping repulsion at all that plastic, all that meat, all that suffocating junk. A sort of asceticism could emerge from deflation, a slow pace of sensuality, and the pursuit of pleasure could become everyone's psychedelic affair: an orgiastic asceticism of precarious communities; a new form of sublimation; a post-sexual sexuality; cultural and symbolic eroticism.

Sensuous Random Compass

Can a compass be sensuous? Can it be random? Obviously not. But this is my suggestion: we need a compass that is able to feel and to vibrate randomly. How can you summarize all this? Following the great late-modern acceleration of the infosphere, the human brain has become unable to process the complexity of the world it has created. Info-neural stimulation has become too intense to be processed consciously and emotionally. So we have entered a dimension of chaos.

The viral proliferation of sub-visible material particles was the final step in this loss of control. But at the same time, the cognitive automaton is generating itself: we are seeing the self-construction of the global interconnection of intelligent artificial units and control devices.

The Automaton is complementary to Chaos.

The sensitive conscious organism enters a spasm: convulsion, suffocation, hyper-excitement, then psycho-deflation. And then?

Neuro-plastic chaosmosis is ongoing. In the random search for a happy evolution beyond the current condition of pain, the compass is sensitivity: neuro-aesthetic harmonization of the rhythm of breathing. But now we must face the neuroplastic dilemma: Can consciousness govern the metamorphosis of consciousness?

In psychedelic substances, as in poetry and insurrection, one finds the answer (approximate, of course, but we are in the domain of uncertainty) to this question. The expansion of sensitive consciousness that some substances make possible provides a way to explore these areas of cognition (and emotion) that are not reduced (so far) to neurophysiological, causal explanation.

Psychedelia enables alterations that interfere with techno-evolution, and simultaneously opens windows on what is beyond the limit of imagination and explores the unimaginable.

Part 3

Fade Out

The Post-Anthropic Evolution of the Psychosphere

The post-anthropic transition is underway: the human domination of the physical and social planet is disintegrating, while the human mind is tending to move into the (techno-) immersive sphere.

Humans are acting like aliens stepping onto an unknown planet whose dynamics they don't fully understand and which they cannot predict: climate cataclysms, rising oceans, water shortages, devastating wars with psychotic backgrounds.

Everywhere the environment turns hostile, tiring, sometimes impractical. While the glaciers at the poles melt, river water is scarce. Drought and floods occur simultaneously in different areas of the world.

Meanwhile, a generation is cognitively forming inside a connective environment: perception changes progressively, while in the networked mind a world is under construction at the intersection of proliferating virtual interactions.

But is the connective dimension completely protected from the crumbling of the physical world? Are those who live their perceptual, affective, economic experience in a virtual dimension impervious to floods, fire, war? I am not so sure, because the infrastructure of the network is not virtual, but heavily physical. This transition of the anthroposphere into the fragile connective dimension needs to be studied.

The first generation that was born inside the networked

space is psychically mutant: the world of desire — that is, tension felt towards the physical — is weakening, while integration with online flows intensifies. Perception, enunciation, and interaction are reformatting on a techno-immersive cognitive level.

With regard to the ongoing shift into the immersive sphere, I would say, incidentally, that the psychedelic is the main line of escape we can imagine: To what extent can psychotropic substances constitute an alternative to electronic flows for enabling immersive experiences? To what extent can psychedelia become a collective line of escape in these times of the evanescence of the human?

The online dimension tends to expand, becoming more pervasive, while access to reality thins out, and the changing mind loses the ability to interact with the physical world while it acquires skill in interacting with the virtual world.

Here emerges a theme that needs to be explored: How is cognitive reframing influencing the psychic sphere? In what sense does the libido change? To what level of intensity does the investment of desire rise?

We are groping in the dark to look for clues to a mutation that is still in progress and in delicate balance on a physical substrate that cannot be ignored: deserts spread, ice melts, even if kids are navigating the Metaverse, watching synthetic panoramas, exploring countless virtual worlds of *Roblox*.

The virtualized post-anthropic environment is not exempt from physical catastrophes, and the digital sphere itself is not independent from physical events, from the degradation of circuits, from the sabotage of power plants or satellites, or from a thousand other physical events that can paralyze it.

How does the conscious and affective organism react to this

mutation, to this inter-penetration of unavoidable physical and mental perceptual levels?

A strange kind of subjectivity is emerging, for which the diagnostic picture inherited from Freud does not work; nor do twentieth-century methods of subjectivation work, since the substance (physical, psychic, cognitive, linguistic) of the human animal has been transformed in a way that is not reducible to the known anthropological models.

Factors of Post-Anthropic Mutation

What factors have affected the psycho-physical organism in recent decades? I would categorize them as follows:

a) Intensification of semiotic emission, acceleration, and intensification of the neuro-informative stimulus; saturation of attention by semiotic stimuli rather than by stimuli coming from the physical body of the surrounding world.

b) Replacement of the speaking (maternal) body by the digital semiotic machine with regard to access to language, language-learning, and affective psycho-genesis.

c) Finally, physical alteration of the environment in which the organism is formed on a psycho-cognitive level, with specific attention to the effects of microplastics in the hormonal functioning of the organism. These effects are affecting sexuality, desire, and fertility.

The experience of the generations born in the new century is increasingly shifting into the connective sphere — less and less bodily experience, more and more semiotic experience. The semiosis, emission, exchange, reception, and interpretation of info-neural stimuli mediated by machines pervade experience, reformatting it down to its psycho-sexual dimensions. In this sense I would speak of pervasive hyper-semiosis.

The singularity of the mother's talking body is replaced by a showing and telling machine. Some Lacanian psychoanalysts blame the disappearance of the father in hyper-expressive environment. However, I think that the most important event is the rarefaction of the bodily, psychic, and linguistic presence of the mother in the perceptive field of the child.

The social emancipation of women and the subsuming of female work into the economic cycle reduce the time of affection available and transform care and education into waged work.

Globalization has entailed a gigantic shift in the affective and bodily presence of the mother. Millions of women are forced to emigrate to carry out care work in distant places, and millions of women are forcibly separated from their children every day at work: the screen is rampant in the attention space of the newborn, whose first impressions have a digital, not a corporeal, substance. Thus a cognitive reformatting and — to an extent that we are not yet able to establish — a neural restructuring is being carried out.

How does this reformatting affect the psycho-sexual sphere? How does it affect the socio-political sphere?

In my opinion, it's not the law of the father but brotherhood that has failed in the post-bourgeois era: solidarity and the pleasure of the relationship with the other have become abstractions that are difficult to experience. The pleasure of the other, the pain of the other, have become distant abstractions, and empathy vanishes.

In this solitude the human organism becomes unassailable,

but at the same time, when exposed to the rigors of the physical and emotional world, the human organism turns extremely fragile. The crystal man, perfectly impermeable to the pain of the other, crumbles upon contact with a planet earth which is increasingly unknown, and upon contact with the inaccessible other from which he distances himself, but which also remains out there, the bearer of possible infection.

But the cause of this loss of brotherhood is not at all to be found in the absence of norms, in the evanescence of the father. The cause lies in the fact that the corporeality of the other has failed in the process of psychic formation.

It was the mother's body that taught us to be fraternal, not the father's law.

If, in the process of linguistic and affective learning, the voice (the point of contact between the flesh and sense) disappears, the sense loses singularity, loses carnality, and what remains is merely operative, functional, and abstract.

The detachment of the child from the mother's body, the replacement of the voice with the linguistic machine, makes the relationship between bodies and the relationship between body and language fragile and therefore precarious.

To conclude this brief survey of the changes that affect the collective and individual psyche in the post-anthropocene transition, it is necessary to consider the effect of the chemical modification of the environment in which the body and mind are formed — not only climate change and the other great processes of de-anthropization, but also the effect of the invasion of the body-mind by mutagenic substances that we are unable to stop. I am thinking, for example, of the issue of microplastics, which have penetrated the food chain and act on the body in a way that is now visible.

According to widely confirmed research, bisphenol and

phthalates, components of microplastics, can interfere with the production of hormones by "imitating" them, deceiving the body and throwing it into crisis. The consequences could affect the thyroid gland and testosterone production, equally important for men and women.

Microplastics (polyfluoroalkyl substances, a.k.a. PFAS) are produced by the chemical industry in the process of making fabrics, paper, and coatings for food containers that are resistant to grease and water, as well as being used for the production of photographic film, fire-fighting foams, and household detergents; they can also be present in paints and varnishes, drugs, and medical aids. It is believed that they contaminate the ecosystem, given that their high thermal and chemical resistance prevents any form of elimination, favoring their accumulation in organisms.

We know of some of their adverse effects on human health, including immune system dysfunction and an increased risk of kidney, testicular, pancreatic, and thyroid cancer, but what interests me most in this context are endocrine disorders. The collapse of male (and possibly female) fertility is the result of a hormonal disturbance that is caused by the penetration of microplastics into the human body and, last but not least, by a reduction in testosterone.

Since the spread of microplastics is not predicted to decrease, we can be sure of the fact that, for physical, medical, as well as cultural reasons, not only will the birth rate decline — and for this we thank the God of microplastics — but sexuality is also destined for a mutation whose signs have long been evident.

Sublimation

David Spiegelhalter's research, published in the book *Sex by Numbers*, reports an impressive reduction in the frequency of sexual intercourse over the past three decades.[1] I believe that in the years following the publication of that book, the trend must have increased because of the catastrophic effect of the pandemic and the subsequent fear of approaching the body, the skin, the lips of the other.

How can we interpret this mutation from the psychic point of view, and then from the cultural point of view? How does the socio-neuro-physical mutation, of which we now have a relatively clear picture, affect the affective sphere, the symbolic one, and ultimately the political one?

There is a Freudian concept that perhaps can help us in this regard: the concept of sublimation, which Freud defines as a displacement of the libidinal drive from the immediacy of sexual pleasure (understood as the discharge of an energy that has physical origin) towards intellectual, spiritual, or aesthetic activities.

In Seminar VII of 1959–60, referring to a brief note contained in Freud's *Three Essays on Sexuality*, Lacan observes how loving pleasure has changed in the transition from the Ancient era to the Christian era:

---

1 David Spiegelhalter (2015) *Sex by Numbers: What Statistics Can Tell Us About Sexual Behavior*, Wellcome Collection.

In a short note in the *Three Essays*, Freud gives us a kind of brief summary in the style of an essay on the difference that strikes us between the love life of antiquity, of pre-Christians, and our own. It resides, he says, in the fact that in antiquity the emphasis was on the instinct itself, whereas we place it on the object.[2]

Lacan means that, in the historical passage from pagan societies to those influenced by Christianity, sexuality was transformed from being essentially centered on the drive itself to being predominantly centered on the object of the drive, on the object of love, so to speak; from the bodily urge to personal affection and desire.

The accentuation of individuality in Christianity, the evolution induced by court cultures, and finally the decisive role that Romanticism plays in culture, aesthetics, and daily life — these are the steps that made possible a transformation of eroticism in the modern sense. This transformation involves, Lacan observes, the emergence of a sense of guilt and a sort of "symbolization of the fantasm (φαντάζω), which is the form on which depends the subject's desire."[3]

There is of course a relationship between sublimation (*Sublimierung*, in Freud) and Repression (*Verdrangung*), but according to what Lacan says, sublimation cannot be reduced to repression.

The hypothesis towards which I am leading you, dear reader, is that we are in the midst of a deep psycho-sexual mutation, as we are witnessing a sort of evacuation of sexuality from the sphere of human experience. The contemporary lessening

---

2   Jacques Lacan (1992) *The Ethics of Psychoanalysis 1959–1960: The Seminar of Jacques Lacan*, Routledge, p. 98.

3   Ibid., p. 99.

of the sexual drive — induced by psychological and physical causes — leads to a systematic sublimation that moves the drive from the sphere of physical contact to the sphere of hyper-semiotic exchange.

The attenuation of the drive, the reformatting of pleasure in the form of a game of language, the ironic multiplication of identity-masking — these are trends that we can already see at work in the sexual (or post-sexual) culture of our time, in the hyper-definition (sometimes pedantically moralistic, sometimes ironic) of sexual desire.

A new ethical dimension emerges at this point: an ethics without a body and without an earth, an ethics of the vanishing simulacrum. This post-anthropocentric culture presents itself as a dispassionate culture, free from bodily passion and from aggressiveness. A world without war, therefore, because the Ares-Aphrodite couple disincarnates, melts, while human history dissolves.

Into Nothingness.

De me fabula narratur
(On Joy, Desire, and Old Age)

Since 2014, when my mother, at the age of ninety-six, entered into a painful agony which led to her death within a year, I have begun to reflect on my life, on the times I have been through, on this exceptionally intense adventure in which I happened to participate, and finally on the precipitation whereby all of humanity seems to be ruined after the defeat of communist internationalism.

Now it is time to give some coherence to my reflection, even if coherence is not easy when fragments of self-analysis are intertwined with the description of large-scale social and anthropological processes. I'm aware that my aging, my personal journey towards death, is intertwined with the aging of the world, with the demographic, economic, and psychological decline of mankind as a whole.

I'm also aware that my analysis of historical processes is influenced by an absolutely personal problem: the painful feeling of impotence, confusion, and incoherence issuing from the decay of my body-brain overlaps with my interpretation of the events of our time.

I often ask the young people who come to listen to my conferences not to take me too seriously, not to believe that what I am saying is true: What I say is just an interpretation of the becoming of the world, and this interpretation is elaborated by a rapidly decaying brain. Do not expect from me the objectivity of the astronomer who deals with stellar constellations or the rigor of the physicist. *De me fabula narratur*, so I won't be objective, because I can't be.

Above all, I do not intend to persuade of my feelings and my predictions any of my readers (who fortunately are not too numerous nor so naïve as to believe that my words contain an indisputable truth). Indeed, I hope they read me with a smile of ironic pity.

I know that my readers are divided into two categories: half of them are my peers, and like me they participated in the adventures of the social movements when the sun of the future had not yet set. The other half are young scholars, artists, and activists who combine the natural energy of age with the awareness that modern hopes are fading. To both I want to say that my intention is not to offer a scientific analysis of biological aging and the decline of human civilization, but a very personal reflection on the psychological and bio-political dimension of aging and the approaching of death.

Lately I have become an expert on a somewhat neglected topic: the decline of the senses. A topic that is full of historical and political implications. Perhaps what human kind is going through is precisely this: a decline in sensitivity, a dulling of the epidermis, and a consequent shrinking of the soul: a becoming-inanimate, therefore, a becoming-fossil of the organic, a becoming-stone of the human heart.

Therefore I dedicate myself with a certain passion to writing about aging, a topic that to most may seem annoying, not out of a pathetic, narcissistic, and self-pitying taste — no, no and no — but because it seems to me that by gazing at my senescent navel I can illuminate some of the trends that define the declining historical era we have entered.

I cannot address the theme of death in an exhaustive way, because it is an inexhaustible theme. Epicurus says that we cannot know anything about death because when we are alive she is not present, and when she is here we are no longer. Nevertheless, philosophy is worth nothing if it is not (also) a reflection on time, and therefore on the decomposition of matter: becoming nothing.

On Happiness, Again

Of course, I can't say what the word "happiness" means. Not because I am scarcely acquainted with it, but because there are no scientific criteria with which to measure it. I can only tell you that I was happy for the simple reason that I felt I was, or rather I believed I was.

Happiness is in fact a perception of oneself that cannot be subjected to objective verification, and which cannot be denied by anyone other than the person talking about themselves. With the word "happiness," I do not mean a feeling of physical well-being or psychological balance, but the feeling of being in tune with one's desire.

The first page of *Anna Karenina* is about (un)happiness: "All happy families are similar to each other; every unhappy family is unhappy in its own way." In *Black Box* (first released in Jerusalem in 1987, in Hebrew, then translated into English in 1988 by Nicholas de Lange), Amos Oz takes the liberty of responding to Tolstoy, and he does so with great elegance:

With all due respect to Tolstoy I want to tell you that for me the opposite is true: unhappy people are generally very conventional, they go forward in their sterile routine with five or six clichés of suffering. On the contrary, happiness is rare, delicate pottery like some kind of Chinese vase, modeled and formed it line after line over the years, so that no two happinesses are the same. There is happiness in the world, even if it is more ephemeral than a dream. Not the satisfaction of approval, not praise or conquest or domination, not the submission or surrender, but the thrill of a fusion.

Joy, Desire, Knowledge

"Happiness," "joy," and "pleasure" are words that evoke different conditions of the harmonious relationship between singular drift and cosmic play. If happiness is the thrill of a fusion, joy is a temporary and intense sensation of exaltation of the soul which does not necessarily coincide with a mobilization of bodily energies. However episodic joy may be, it leaves a trace that is not lost, and which can be found and reactivated when the conditions of joy have dissolved. There can be joy also in the absence of pleasure, and even in conditions of suffering. There is a joy in suffering that Dostoevsky exalts in some of his novels. There is a joy in suffering that Christianity has elevated to the ethics of salvation.

Pleasure, linked to the dimension of sensuality, manifests itself as the relaxation that follows the desiring tension. There can be pleasure without joy. There can be pleasure in abjection and pain.

But there is no joy if there is no desire.

Desire is essentially projection, a reaching out, an expansion of the singular being that projects.

In our times, desire is displaced to the techno-digital dimension of virtual immersion, and bodies are secluded in the connective dimension.

Can joy be turned into a pure game of language?

Can joy be disjoined from corporeality?

I think old age is the condition for understanding this mutation, which is based on the transfer of desire from the bodily to the semiotic sphere.

Old age is perceived in many different forms, but I would define it as a slow deactivation of the relationship between desire and pleasure.

Desire does not disappear when biological time erodes physical energy; what fades away is the ability to experience pleasure.

At this point, desire may turn into torment, unless we learn the subtle art of sublimation, of irony and lightness.

As the digital age is marked by the de-sexualization of desire, the art of sublimation is crucial for the evolution of the human species.

Aging is essentially the inexorable weakening of the ability to experience pleasure, because little by little the physical conditions that make it possible disappear. Not just the sensual pleasure of caressing other bodies and enjoying them erotically. But also the simple pleasure of walking. Even if you can still walk, the painful heaviness of the flesh that loses elasticity prevents the pleasure of feeling the autumnal smell of the air.

Attention inevitably focuses on the pain in the hips and the tremor of the legs and on the arthritis that makes the knee fragile.

Can there be joy in old age?

A Zen sage quoted by Daniel Suzuki states: "In the mind of the beginner many possibilities, in the mind of the expert few."

In fact, knowledge comes with a narrowing of the field of desire. When we know, when we have come to know, then the adventure of desire is over.

The soul remembers, the materialistic soul that lies in the neuronal circuits designed by the pleasure and suffering of the body — that soul remembers.

The epidermis is the memory of caresses, and naturally it is also the memory of violence. In our age the epidermis records loneliness, exploitation, humiliation.

However, the soul does not lose track of joy.

In the digital age, the epidermis is becoming sensitive to techno-immersive perception. Will the techno-immersive evolution of sensitivity allow us to transmigrate beyond the layers of horror and traumas?

Will the soul be able to preserve the memory of past happiness, and to recreate its possibility? In "Goodbye to the Mezzogiorno," recalling the years spent on the island of Ischia, Auden writes:

Though one cannot always
Remember exactly why one has been happy,
There is no forgetting that one was.

Post Scriptum

As you have had the patience to follow me this far, you have probably understood that the desertion that I have been praising is ultimately a desertion from being. The abandonment of the primacy of (human) Being over Becoming (other). The ironic abandonment of the (failed) experiment of the civilization created by the intelligent and passionate animal that has destroyed both itself and the planet.

6 December 2022

REPEATER BOOKS

is dedicated to the creation of a new reality. The landscape of twenty-first-century arts and letters is faded and inert, riven by fashionable cynicism, egotistical self-reference and a nostalgia for the recent past. Repeater intends to add its voice to those movements that wish to enter history and assert control over its currents, gathering together scattered and isolated voices with those who have already called for an escape from Capitalist Realism. Our desire is to publish in every sphere and genre, combining vigorous dissent and a pragmatic willingness to succeed where messianic abstraction and quiescent co-option have stalled: abstention is not an option: we are alive and we don't agree.